One Kiss

One Kiss

Michelle Ashton

Copyright © 2025 by Michelle Ashton
All rights reserved. No part of this book may be reproduced in any manner whatsoever without written permission except in the case of brief quotations embodied in critical articles and reviews.
First Printing, 2025

I dedicate this book to all of humanity, the animals, and the planet.

Happy Valentine's Day, my gift of love for the entire Universe.

This book started as a therapeutic tool for my emotions during one of my life's hardest, most transformative and fulfilling journeys. What I uncovered along the way was both terrifying and magical. I made it to the other side, and my life has never been better. Everyone should take a journey back to their authentic self.

This first entry was made on Tuesday, April 18th, 2023, after realising my Spiritual awakening was occurring. It includes the history and interactions between Noah and me up until then.

- When a Spiritual awakening occurs, it is such a profound transformation that changes your whole life perspective. You question all the beliefs you previously held, see the bigger picture, and realise your potential.

Dear Journal,

Sebastian, my younger brother, was the one to bring us together. Firstly, he took me to Noah's place of work, and secondly, the times he had orchestrated catch-ups at his house. Seb was the first one to notice how similar we are. What a beautiful memory that it was my little bro, who I love so much; the thought warms my heart. I just felt so comfortable in Noah's presence. Oh my gosh, I used to call him babe, just like I would call a partner or a girlfriend, not a guy friend. How embarrassing; I didn't even know him well. I thought I didn't; I had no idea at the time. I see this man as well as I understand myself.

It is so strange; we were acquaintances in the same social circle. Thank goodness we didn't lock eyes before. Can you imagine the upheaval in our lives? I can't even begin to contemplate, I was married; Noah was married. I remember seeing him at a friend's wedding in Lake Como in September 2018. Multiple events surrounded the wedding; we were both in attendance with our now ex-spouses. I honestly don't even think we spoke two words at those celebrations.

30th December 2019 - Noah comes to Moonstruck in Byron Bay with his ex-wife and two other friends. I was there with my ex-husband Ian, who had rented the property for the holidays. We chatted that day. Noah, to me, was merely his ex-wife's handsome, lovely husband.

Our paths didn't cross again until Sunday, August 28, 2022. Seb had booked a restaurant in Cronulla. He had moved from the eastern suburbs to this southern suburb of Sydney only six months ago. Seb and I both found ourselves single after failed marriages. He is treating me to a late lunch with his friends; they are such a lovely couple, and I really enjoy their company. Seb said a mate had been to this restaurant the previous night and that it was really good.

We all rock into Zimzala; I bump into Noah, who works there. I was shocked to see him in Sydney; he lived in Byron Bay with his wife. I ask him where she is; he tells me they broke up. I feel so sad for both of them; they, too, had been together for a long time, I think it was 13 years. I was with my ex-husband for 15 years; I had not long gotten a divorce. It's heartbreaking; I feel such compassion for them. It's something you wouldn't wish on your own worst enemy.

At lunch, we discussed my ideal partner's qualities list. I wasn't ready for another relationship but determined to get it right next time. I'm not going to fall in lust again. I decided to list qualities I was truly after, so when I was ready, I was armed. While the four of us were at the table discussing the list, my perfect guy was right over there, in the same restaurant; crazy hey, seriously? Still, to this day, the thought blows my mind.

Seb, too, is such an empathetic Soul and, unfortunately, knows first-hand how devastating the ending of a marriage can be. Seb decides to Invite Noah back for a drink at his place. Seb's friends head home, and Seb, Noah and I hang out back at my bro's, drinking, chatting and doing drugs for over 12 hours. That's what drugs do; a 12-hour drug-fuelled session flies by. One minute, you're having your first line of cocaine and the next, the sun is coming up. Noah and I are just friends; there was utterly nothing to it, just another drug-fuelled night as I have had with other mates.

Afterwards, I sent an Instagram message to his ex to say how sorry I was to hear about them. She messaged back and was shocked we had caught up, but she was nice to me and always has been. I offered that if it made her feel more comfortable, I would ask my bro to steer clear. My question went unanswered in her next reply, so I figured it didn't bother her much. Seb and Noah are now friends. They hung out a few times before Noah and my subsequent encounter.

On Christmas Day 2022, Seb takes me for another beautiful lunch at Manta in Woolloomooloo. We are with the same lovely couple from the Zimzala lunch. This time, we started at midday with the drinks overflowing, and by the time lunch had come to a close, I was pretty hammered. I was staying at Seb's, so we decided to kick back at his pad; we were being driven about a forty-five-minute journey to his house. We dropped off his friends and continued the long drive home. Seb couldn't wait and had a line of cocaine in the back of the car; he offered me one. I decline and say "I'll wait until we are back at yours." Seb called Noah to see if he wanted to come over for a drink. We arrive back from lunch, and shortly after, I hear a knock at the door. I open, hug Noah, and say "Hi, babe; Merry Christmas." I feel such ease around this guy.

I think it's around 7 am, and once again, another drug-fuelled night flies by. I tell the guys I must go to bed and lie down. I was smashed. I go to the bathroom and remove my makeup; I walk into the kitchen where Seb and Noah are and ask my bro to help take my earrings out. I go to bed, and I hear Noah say to Seb, I better head too, and he goes home.

It's a week later, it's New Year's Eve. We are ready for another party. We have a WhatsApp group message connecting Noah, Seb, and another of his mates; we are discussing the late afternoon lunch we planned at Zimzala. It's another drunken lunch with many of us eating, drinking and laughing. Noah is working and just finished his shift. The group is leaving to go to Seb's friend's house. I go into the bathroom and tell Noah to come in; I then take half of an ecstasy pill and hand the other half to him, which he takes with a sip of water. I go to the friend's home, and Noah says he is going home to freshen up and will then come to join us. At the party, Seb says, "What about Noah? He could be your once-a-week hook-up." I just wrote it off and said "We are 100% just mates; it's too bloody complicated being in the same social circle." That's what I used to think I wanted: just a once-a-week liaison. Really, who was I kidding? I've never had casual sex in my whole life. Was I going to start now as a 47-year-old divorcee?

Back at the friend's house, Seb and I are getting nervous. One of the people in the group is a police officer, and we have to be discreet. We want to be able to get high without worrying about getting caught. We take the party back to Seb's house and tell Noah to meet us there. Seb's friends rock up throughout the night and more in the morning. Even in the daylight hours, we are undeterred. Noah leaves sometime in the morning, and the party continues without him. I am so high. It may have been 7 or 8 am when I called Dad. I say "If I die, it's Seb's fault." Dad laughed; he knew we were all high and asked what we had taken; he began chatting with another of Seb's friends, as I was almost speechless. This party is getting out of control; the amount of drugs going around is just pure insanity, even for a seasoned drug taker. I am supposed to stay at Seb's, but I must leave. I organised an Uber, collected my things, and ran out the door. No one notices I've left until hours later when Seb sends me a text message; it doesn't wake me. I took Valium, which usually does the trick after a big night. Not today; I'm still sleepless and high as a kite.

January 2nd, 2023: I dreamt about Noah. It was strange, and it involved a Vietnamese soup. I love a good Pho. He had made it for me and presented the bowl. I looked inside, and there was a massive shrimp. My first thought was that I'm allergic to crustaceans. I know now that dreams have Spiritual meanings. The shrimp in a dream can represent life's pleasures. The following day, I was curious and petrified at the same time, but here goes: I texted Noah asking him if he wanted to catch up at his place. I thought he would be a beautiful first hook-up after ex-husband Ian; I hadn't slept with another man in 17 years. Noah is so kind and, not to mention, totally hot. I think the last time I was this nervous about sex was when I lost my virginity.

Wednesday, January 4th, 2023, was the day my life changed forever. Noah looked at me deep in the eyes. It was the strangest look like he was seeing right through me. His eyes became transparent and hypnotic. I've never experienced a look like this. At the time, I didn't even think, let alone understand, that it was Soul recognition.

I thank him for looking me in the eyes; not surprisingly, he was always going to; it was Divine timing. Noah asks me if I want to stay over; thanks, but I better go home. I think that's a bit much; I'm determined to keep this connection with Noah simply as my very special mate. I just got out of a 15-year relationship. I leave, and just as I'm almost home, Noah texts, saying he had a nice time. I'm driving, so I can't text. I called him back, and we chatted; neither mentioned the eye connection; I couldn't understand it myself. We also spoke the following day; we still didn't discuss the eye connection.

The following week, I'm obsessing like never before, waiting for some contact. Finally, he texts, YAY! We are texting back and forth; I am shocked at how similar our backgrounds are, even including our exes; this is freaky.

12th January 2023 – It's Noah's birthday today; he is turning 48, eight and a half months before it's my turn. I texted him a happy birthday, and we shared a few pleasant exchanges. I enjoy learning about this man, his likes, his dislikes. What is it about him that I find so mesmerising? I can't put my finger on it; he is ridiculously handsome, kind and ever so cool, but it's something else. I need to be careful; I can't get enough. No matter how much attention he gives me, I want more and more.

Saturday, 14th January, 2023, Noah texted asking if I wanted to catch up. I have had a few vinos tonight; he caught me at a good time. Yeah, why not? He had also been drinking, so I went into my safe and pulled out a bag of cocaine. I then jump into an Uber, making the long journey to his place. When I arrived, I walked inside and hugged him very strangely. It seemed as if I didn't want to let go; he asked if I was okay. How embarrassing; that was not acting cool in the slightest. We drink, we chat, we do drugs. He started kissing me. I was so attracted to this man. This is a passion I have never felt before. Just him touching me is magnetic; it feels like electricity is coming through his hands. He then says "I love you," but I am distrusting of men. I think he is either drunk, high, playing games or all of the above. I look at him blankly, and he then says, "Oh, I love this." It's a little awkward, but knowing what I know now, thank goodness. I can only imagine how much harder it would be if I had spent more time with him.

The energy in the room is overwhelming; Noah says, "I'm really high." "Me too," I was so relieved. I put my bra back on and hear "Hang on," but I'm too fast. I can't get out of there quick enough. In the Uber, I text him to thank him for a beautiful night. The energy is too intense in his presence, but I am still so drawn to this man. We share many texts back and forth; the long Uber ride home flies by. We are still texting each other into the wee hours of the morning. I am starting to realise how much we have in common.

Seriously, this is so bizarre. Is he just in agreeance and full of shit?

Over the following weeks, I am sending bizarre text messages to this man. I have no idea where it is coming from; I have no control over what I send. I re-read them, dying from embarrassment. I didn't understand at the time these were triggers, and it did not stop there. I sent him a sexual audio recording of myself; I am mortified; I hadn't even done that with my ex-husband. I do not understand myself at this point; who am I? Why am I acting like this?

- A trigger stirs up deep emotions, fears, wounds, pain, insecurities, ego or beliefs and especially fears of rejection or abandonment.

Monday, 30th January 2023 - Seb tells me he can't attend the Red Hot Chilli Peppers concert. I am bummed; I had been looking forward to this for months. We were supposed to be going with a group of his friends. He says, "You still go; why don't you invite Noah?" Seb thinks he might enjoy the concert too. My brother doesn't know we have hung out previously, just the two of us. I don't see the point in telling him; it's messy with our mutual friends, and honestly, there isn't much to tell. We have hung out twice on our own, the magical night on the 4th of January, then the drug-fuelled night when I left early. We hadn't been on a date, it wasn't like that.

Saturday, February 4th, 2023: I'm so excited; the night is finally here. Not only do I get to see Red Hot Chilli Peppers in concert, but I also get to hang out with Noah. We are going as mates in a group; this isn't a date, though I like spending time with him.

I pick up Noah at 4 pm; he has his sunglasses on today, phew. Whenever he looks at me deep in the eyes, it's so intense, and other people are around us tonight. We make a pit stop to load up on drugs for the night. We take four ecstasy tablets and a bag of cocaine with us. We then dropped the car off at my place and got an Uber to Seb's friend's, where they had drinks waiting for us. They have organised a Hummer limousine to take the group to the stadium. We leave a little stash of our drugs and head off in the limo, continuing the drinking on the way. Minutes before we arrive, we take some ecstasy; it will take effect whilst we are inside the concert.

The friends have organised a private suite; the drinks are free and flowing. There is also food, but I don't touch it. Not only am I drinking, this ecstasy is extreme. I am so smashed, acting like a little girl, and being so needy, I desperately want his attention. I don't know what is coming over me. No one else in the stadium exists; I only have eyes for him. Please notice me. No, he is just horrible to me. He is so horrendous that he makes me cry.

On the way back, in the Hummer, we are arguing, and I don't want anyone to hear us. Therefore, I am speaking quietly. Out of nowhere, Noah says, "I'm not your boyfriend." What is he talking about? Where did that come from? Having a connection is one thing, but a boyfriend? Cool your jets, buddy. You would be very lucky to be my boyfriend, mate. I think this to myself, but I don't say that; I confusingly look at him. Seriously, who am I? He is so mean to me, and I keep my cool.

I try to say something else, but I don't make sense; I am so smashed on drugs. Noah says condescendingly, "I can't even understand you." I now make some bloody sense; "Would you like me to get you an Uber?" We arrive back at the friend's, and he flees immediately, leaving me outside on the street, drunk and on drugs. At this point, I am so messy; I haven't been this smashed my entire life. I cannot even book my own Uber to get home; thank goodness some of Seb's friends helped me collect my keys and get me inside the Uber. On the way, I call my brother in tears; I have no idea what to say to him. I arrive home still on the phone and jump out. I leave my bag in the Uber. Fortunately, the friendly driver saw this and beeped his horn to get my attention. I would have been in no state to deal with this. I finally stumbled in my door and sent Noah a message.

Hi beautiful, I'm at home I'm
sorry if I gott a bit upset I
thing fvjoik. 8'dipstick

I'm still in dioxin bits cool?
I'm ok get over it.

I thought we were very
hspecial metex

What a trigger to be in that state and not be able to take care of myself, especially as a woman. I am so lucky the Uber driver handed me my bag; I have no idea what I would have done. I couldn't even speak, walk or see straight, let alone organise a locksmith at that hour. Disgraceful. This was a massive lesson.

On Monday, February 6th, 2023, Noah visited Byron Bay to see some old friends. I texted him to ask how he was, suggested we could still be friends and wished him a great holiday. He texted back right away in agreement. All good mates it is.

Saturday, 11th February 2023, this morning, this afternoon and this evening, I sent some more random texts. What am I doing? Who am I? Where is Michelle?

It's the morning of February 12, 2023; I'm up early, in a great mood and ready for my busy day. Like many of us, Noah uses the do not disturb feature on his phone; you know you can send a text, and they will receive it later when they wake up. I send my welcome to today morning meditation; it's beautiful, and I have been listening to it for years. I add that I am in a fantastic mood and that meditation is a great way to start the day. He is on holiday and has plenty of time for meditation. Straight away, he texts back. He isn't impressed and texts some horrible things. I am not backing down today or letting anyone disrupt my terrific mood. I am not rude to him; I just nicely put him in his place. He hasn't seen this side of Michelle. I must have ruffled his feathers as he texted, *Pls leave me alone.* I respond, *Ditto.* He wasn't expecting that; he is getting hot under the collar. How does he respond? Then my phone goes, beep, beep. I read *I'm blocking u.* No one is putting a damper on my day, especially not rude Noah Henley. I answer instantly; I'm not sure I have ever typed so quickly; I am pissed, but I text, *How lovely*. How else should one respond to such childish behaviour? My phone goes beep beep again, yet another text from him: *You don't respect my boundaries, so....* I am done with this rubbish; I do not reply; I have a busy day to get on with. I put my music on, danced to return to my previous mood, and tried to forget about the silly quarrel.

It took me a couple of weeks to get past the unkindness of our last interaction when one of Seb's friends texted me asking for Noah's number; they wanted to go to the restaurant for their birthday breakfast. He knows them, and I know he won't mind, so I pass on his number and text him, *just giving you the heads up, Seb's friend will be calling you for a booking.* I don't hear anything back; that's weird. I figure he is just busy. A few days and messages later, still nothing; mmmm, this is not like Noah. Is he ok? I am starting to worry. I call him, but it goes straight to voicemail.

I'm getting concerned as he is going through a tough time after his break-up. I called my brother, "I can't get hold of Noah. Has anyone seen him recently? I'm worried, I haven't heard from him." Seb answers, "Yes, he seems fine." I'm glad he is fine and alive, so why is he not answering me? Numerous messages and phone calls go unanswered; did he block me? No, it can't be true. It was so trivial, and he was the unkind one; if anyone should have blocked anyone, it should have been me blocking him.

On Friday, 10th March 2023, a friend, Lilith and her long-term partner, Andrew, invited me for an early dinner. The couple have moved into an ultra-lux apartment in the prestigious Knox St Double Bay. They are waiting for their multi-million dollar Bondi Beach penthouse to be completed. They suggest going to Margaret in Double Bay, right down the road from their pad, to show off their new digs. They are trying to persuade me to return to theirs for a drink. Andrew leaves the restaurant before us, leaving Lilith, and I to have dessert and more drinks. Lilith is still trying to persuade me to come back. I'm just not feeling it. I don't want to be rude; I say I'm tired and book my Uber. I took a photo with my friend of 20 years and posted it to Instagram. Fifteen minutes later, I was in the Uber, and on the way home, I called my brother; I wouldn't mind catching up with him. He isn't picking up; he has been partying a little too much recently and wanted an early night; therefore, I'm happy he doesn't answer. Hopefully, he is getting some much-needed rest.

Saturday, 11th March 2023, It's very early; the sun is just about to appear. Seb is calling, and I answer. I hope all is well. "What's wrong, mate? Are you ok?" He replies you won't believe what happened. As you called, I was in the shower, about to go to bed. I hear loud banging on my door; then someone walks around my property calling out my name and knocking on the windows; what the heck? I rush downstairs. It's Noah. He is drunk and is with some girl they want to come in. He said he couldn't call because he lost his phone. I invite them in; they are so drunk they are bashing against the walls as they walk down the hallway. We drank all night and took so many lines of coke; there goes my quiet night.

I have now had it; how rude. I worry about Noah. He doesn't answer my texts or calls but takes some chick to Seb's to party all night. I spent a lot of time with him. How did he know I wouldn't be there? Did he not care? Did he want to parade some girl in front of my face, in my bro's home, because he knows he isn't aware of our special friendship? Does he think I will put up with this atrocious behaviour? Oh, I am so pissed, this is so disrespectful, and I was hoping Seb was taking a night off the drugs. He has crossed the line; I will not allow this to happen again. I cry and tell my brother everything except the eye connection; I do not understand this myself. I beg him not to say anything; I don't want to give Noah the satisfaction of knowing he has gotten under my skin.

Seb is so understanding; I knew he would be; he is also shocked and pissed off at Noah. Seb is very protective over his sister, especially now that I am on my own; even so, he promises me that he will not tell Noah and keep my secret.

What have I done? How could I have chosen someone as mean-spirited as this man to give all of myself to? It is the most beautiful and sacred possession a woman has. I shared mine with disrespectful Noah; I am devastated; I wish I could turn back the clock.

My brother has another phone number that he uses for naughty purposes, so I ask him to forward a message to Noah for me; I am making sure he receives it this time.

Hi Noah, I am unsure if you are getting my text messages if I'm blocked or being ignored; either way, it's not very nice, and I honestly do not know why you would find it necessary. I think I have been more than understanding. My bro said you were there last night with a girl. It's none of my business what you are doing and with whomever, but bringing them into my brother's home to party all night at his expense is not cool. I will not be treated in that manner. I deserve respect. Michelle

Even after Noah's despicable behaviour, I'm still obsessing over him. It's ridiculous, pure insanity; he is on my mind non-stop. Every waking moment and at night, I dream about him. I am going crazy. What is happening? Time goes so slowly; every minute feels like an hour, every hour feels like a day, and every week feels like a month. Time is almost at a standstill. I can't shut my mind off. Noah, Noah, Noah, I'm obsessed. I check his focus status every evening to see if he is safe at home in bed. It's my little connection to him; I know it's sick, but I find it soothing. Why am I so worried about this man? What's happening to me? I watch Instagram tarot readings all the time; it's become a hobby; how tragic.

My emotions are up, down and everywhere. One day, I was fine and dandy mere moments before, and then, out of nowhere, I got furious and slammed my hand down on my steering wheel. The strange thing is, I don't even have that emotion anymore; I cannot remember the last time I lost my cool. Where is this coming from? Also, I am sad when I am happy or laughing moments before. Tears, then a minute later, laughing uncontrollably, I don't tell anyone about this; I think I'm going crazy. I am crying myself to sleep at night, having such weird phenomena. One night, I was crying so much, then suddenly, I felt like someone was there, I couldn't see anyone. I'm unsure what I think is lying in bed next to me; it feels comforting. I remember asking can you please stay until I go to sleep. The tears were so bad that my face was drenched, and my pillow was soaked. I didn't dare get up to get tissues; I was afraid whatever lies next to me might leave. I'm completely screwed at this point. I have never been so scared of my mind; I seriously think I have lost it. The complete and utter madness continues; I am talking to myself, I am comforting myself with hugs, and I'm crying myself to sleep at night. I am non-stop thinking about Noah, even sexually. I am obsessing over someone I hardly know. My only conclusion is it must be some weird attachment issue that is sending me crazy. Am I attached because he is the only man, other than my ex-husband, I have been intimate with in 17 years? Please, God, what is happening to me? If this continues, I will have to go to a mental institution. I don't have time to deal with this. I have a start-up I have been working on for years, and my business baby needs my full and undivided attention. Please mind, please don't leave me now.

I am, honestly, so scared. I am single, live alone, and have bills to pay. I don't have anyone else to pick up the slack If I need a break to look after my mental health. I am so close to launching my wedding dress label. I have worked on this for years, so much money has been poured into this. I have no staff, and even if I could afford them, it's quite a new concept; no one can get inside my head to understand my vision. I don't even understand my mind at this point. What happens If I am drugged up in a mental institution? I have everything riding on this; I have spent years researching and working in this industry. I have complete faith in my abilities if only my mind doesn't desert me now.

I don't dare tell my brother what is happening; firstly, I don't want to worry him, and secondly, I don't want to believe I'm going crazy. I turn to Google. I put in all my symptoms, and the same thing keeps popping up; the dots start connecting, but I keep researching as I'm in disbelief. Google is alluding to what I am going through is the Twin Flame journey.

I had only heard of this once before; a psychic had suggested that maybe my ex-husband Ian was a Soulmate or even a Twin Flame, and that was why I was finding it so hard to let go and move on following the marriage breakdown. I had heard of a Soulmate but didn't have the darnedest what a Twin Flame was until a few days ago. I now understand I had suffered from Stockholm syndrome after the break up with Ian. We had very little in common. A generational gap meant we didn't share the same taste in music or movies. We didn't have the same values or beliefs. I couldn't stand when he would say something racist or put others down. Even family or friends of ours who were doing well in life, hell, even long-time friends of his. He could never be genuinely happy for anyone; that would always ensure an argument. I love to see people thrive, especially my loved ones, and I am vehemently adamant about equality. I also love the beach, playing games, particularly arcade games, and going on rides at theme parks. I went to a waterpark for my 35th birthday and loved every minute; I'm a big kid at heart, and Ian would prefer to while away his time inside a fancy restaurant. He is into politics; I'm into Spirituality. I like to listen to music; he would have the news on the box all day, every day. Even if he wasn't watching, it was on in the background; this was incredibly uplifting during the Covid lockdowns. Before Ian, I had been a vegetarian for some time in my 20s; Ian eats steak every night of the week, which is interchanged with either chips or vegetables. Heck, we didn't even like the same scents. I'm obsessed with coconut. It reminds me of the beach. It repulsed Ian. I couldn't even have the fragrance in a body wash; he would tell me it smelt like a dirty woman's private parts. I think the only thing we did have in common is we both liked to get smashed. With nothing in common, no wonder we did more of that. If all that isn't enough to discourage the psychic's suggestion. There was never any eye connection with Ian; only those who have experienced this will understand Soul recognition is magical.

Let me explain a Twin Flame: its purpose, journey, roles, and mission.

A Twin Flame is the most profound Spiritual connection one can have. Unlike Soulmates, where you can have multiple in your lifetime, you only have one Twin Flame. Soulmates are two different Souls that share an extraordinary bond. A Twin Flame is your mirror, the same Soul split in two. Soulmate connections are miraculous, but rare Twin Flame connections are entirely on another level.

Spiritual growth is the primary purpose of a Twin Flame; encountering yours speeds up your growth, and if you work hard enough, you can reach Enlightenment. Your Twin Flame holds a mirror or shines a light on everything that needs to be healed. All your wounds, fears and deepest insecurities. It shouldn't be confused with being toxic; they do this from a place of unconditional love. In another physical being, it is your Soul helping you heal and guiding you to true self-love.

The Twin Flame journey leads you back to your authentic self. It is challenging, harrowing, heart-wrenching, heart-opening, and profoundly transformative. This Divinely guided journey is the hardest yet most fulfilling, with the final destination being Twin Flame union.

Twin Flames take on the roles of runner or chaser; you decide these roles before rebirth. The chaser characteristically has abandonment issues, whilst the runner has maturity issues. I am the chaser, and Noah is the runner. It is said that during the journey, it is common for the roles to switch so that each twin can experience both roles. One Twin is the Divine feminine energy, the DF, usually but not always the more Spiritual twin who awakens to the connection first; the other Divine masculine, the DM, is the Matrix un-awakened twin who denies the connection. Each twin encompasses both energies, but because of childhood traumas, they are unbalanced. The Divine feminine can have hyperactive masculine energy and vice versa. This has nothing to do with physical gender; it's a term to describe energy. Even in same-sex couples, one will predominantly embody the Divine feminine energy and the other Divine masculine. So again, this has little to do with gender. The feminine is about being; the energy is loving, nurturing and compassionate. While the masculine is about doing, action-based, taking charge energy. These energies must be balanced for each twin to complement each other; the Twin Flame journey shows us the way.

Serving humanity is the mission of Twin Flames; this loving union inspires everyone to live from a place of unconditional love. They raise the planet's vibration and humanity's frequency, bringing peace, love and happiness to Earth.

I am shocked and confused. Could this be true? Am I indeed a Twin Flame, and is Noah my Divine counterpart? I have so many questions. There is no denying that all my symptoms match the Twin Flame journey, but still, I am sceptical. Is this just a bunch of baloney? I found a professional Twin Flame reader. I have a booking on Thursday; frankly, this cannot come soon enough.

Thursday, 13th April, It is just over 2 Months since he may have blocked me. My appointment with the reader is here; she specialises in Twin Flames. I feel silly talking to her about this; I don't give too much information as it all seems gibberish. She takes names, dates of birth and a few other details. She added my details and said yes, I am a Twin Flame. Next is Noah's turn. Yes, we are both Twin Flames. WTF, she can see how shocked I am; I am still unconvinced. She deals with this daily; knows I doubt her professional opinion, and doesn't need to prove her psychic abilities to me. I am told to find another professional who offers past life regression. Great, I think, yes, a second opinion is what

I need. I frantically look online; I need to get to the bottom of this nonsense. I managed to get a cancellation from a reputable one the following day. Yes, I can come to an appointment tomorrow. I will drop everything to find out what is happening to me.

This is serious now; I set my phone to a private number and call Noah. I desperately need to speak with him to find out if he is having any of the same symptoms. A woman answers his phone. "Is Noah available, please?" "Who is calling?" "Michelle," I then hear her announce to Noah, "It's Michelle." "Michelle who?" "Michelle Ashton." I listen to her recite again to Noah, and then she responds, "No, no, he isn't here "and then hangs up on me. I was in tears, and soon after, I received a text message from him: *stop contacting me, we are no longer friends.* Then he sends another text with precisely the same message: *stop contacting me, we are no longer friends.*

I was so upset I called my brother. Can you believe Seb. I just tried to call Noah, but a woman answered, and even my first name wouldn't suffice. I could hear him, and then she said no, he wasn't here and hung up; I just wanted to ask him something. He then sends me this text message, stop contacting me we are no longer friends. What's wrong with this guy? He loses his cool in a hot second.

14th April 2023, I had my appointment for past life regression today. It was a lot harder than I thought it would be. I only got to uncover three past lives; the lovely woman asked me all sorts of questions to find out what era I was in, such as the clothing, what the houses looked like, etc. Do you need to be a history buff? I'm blonde at the best of times.

I don't know the answers, but she says that's okay, let's keep going. The following past life is where we have to stop; I am too distraught. I am a man in this past life, and I know I have done something terrible to my wife; the tears are indescribable. I don't know what I have done, but it's awful. I am in jail, and I am so sorry. I keep repeating what have I done, I'm so sorry. I'm so sorry. It's too much. The therapist is so lovely, and she announced that we would stop here and that she would come in on Sunday for me to pick up where we left off. God bless her.

Sunday, 16th April 2023. I was feeling more confident in my past life regression appointment today. I knew how the appointment would run and what to expect. I was determined to find out the answers I came looking for. Today, I uncovered another six previous lives, and there were no tears, nothing upsetting. These past lives were just full of joy. It's just a feeling you get, well I did. You feel when people you know are there with you. You are different people, so it's a feeling. You know who is part of your Soul family. In one past life, I was asked what I was doing. I reply that I am at a party and eating lots of food; there is so much, it's really yummy, and I'm dancing; out of nowhere, I start laughing uncontrollably. I am asked what's funny, and I say it's Salma, my best friend, cracking me up.

I am stunned it's true; I sense Noah in two past lives. I was so happy in both; I cannot explain my happiness and contentment. First, we live in the country; I have no idea how many children we have as there are so many little clothes on the washing line. I am surprised there was time to do anything else in this lifetime. In another past life, we were at the beach with our two children and dressed, with no shoes on. I don't know why we are clothed. I get asked if it is cold and don't know the answer. I can't work it out. I now understand my love of the beach goes back further than this lifetime.

These last two appointments have been the best Spiritual therapy; who knows if you have Karma to repay that doesn't even belong to you in this lifetime? The tears that came with uncovering my jail sentence were so real I had done something ghastly. I was so upset and remorseful; it's not even in my lifetime, and I can't fathom how I could have done something so terrible. How else could I have shed Karma and tears for something I had no recollection of?

Tuesday, 18th April 2023 - Today was the best day of my life so far. This is a day that will etched in my memory forever. I have realised that my Spiritual awakening is occurring. This date will be celebrated yearly; it's even more important to me than a birthday. I will call it my Spiritual birthday. I need to start documenting my days; when I have time, I will journal. Yes, that's what I need to do; yes, that's what I will do.

Love, Michelle Ashton

Wednesday, 19th April 2023

Dear Journal,

I'm on the treadmill at the gym this morning, which overlooks Princes Highway. I look at a hearse that has a coffin inside. I make the sign of the cross to ask for Divine protection, but all I can think about is ego death. Why am I thinking of such a thing? Why did this enter my mind? The very next morning, after realising my Spiritual awakening was occurring. My mind is powerful; it reveals things that need my attention.

This evening, I had dinner with Seb at the Cronulla RSL. I don't tell him that I have realised my awakening is occurring. I love my brother, but Seb isn't Spiritual and will think I'm completely nuts. Everything I've told him about Noah up until now, I wished I hadn't. First, I didn't realise what was happening; I just thought Noah was being a big jerk. Second, when I got confirmation and tried to call him, I didn't realise the depth of our connection. You only realise this upon awakening. I know how much Seb loves me, and I'm sure he would try his hardest to grasp the concept. I know anyone who isn't on this journey would have a tough time understanding as it's hard to comprehend when you're on it. I'm living through it, and I still think, WTF? I tell my brother I'm going through Spiritual stuff and thank God for bringing Noah into my life, but I don't say anymore.

Love, Michelle Ashton

Saturday, 22nd April 2023

Dear Journal,

I called a girlfriend, Salma, and told her I wanted to see her. I desperately need to talk, and she needs to keep an open mind. I got into my car, and my Spiritus Stones crystal protection bracelet broke and went everywhere. I had been wearing this forever and didn't even knock it; I loved that bracelet. When I arrived, I told her it was upsetting, and I wondered if that meant I shouldn't speak with her; she told me the meaning of protection bracelets breaking. It absorbs the negative energy and protects the wearer from harm.

Wow, the synchronicities; I know what I will divulge to her. She could think I have lost it and call my brother, so I watered it down. Salma, I believe I have met my Twin Flame. She has questions trying to understand this concept. I explain as much as possible, including the bizarre texting and feeling his energy. Twin Flames share identical energy; they are connected through their chakras. I feel when he is happy, sad, angry, or in ecstasy, which is a tough one to bear, as I know it's not me he is with, and even sleepless. I wish he could get on top of the latter; I am so tired. I am not embarrassed to tell Salma; I have known her since I was 12, and we have been best friends for 35 years. I also told her I am in love with him. It doesn't matter what he did. There is nothing that could make me look at him differently. I protect myself by saying I don't care about the outcome, but the truth is, I'm besotted; I have fallen for that man, hook, line and sinker. Love, Michelle Ashton

Tuesday, 25th April 2023

Dear Journal,

I had a follow-up appointment today with the Twin Flame reader. I asked if she could tell me how Noah was, as I wanted to ensure he was okay. She connects with him and assures me all is well. He has no clue about our connection, but he is happy. Then she laughs and says she hasn't had this one before; he feels sexy. A few days ago, I gave him a nickname that I will call him for the rest of my life: Adonis. I wonder if he felt it. I'm trying to send loving energy and keep my vibration high, which is hard nowadays. I have read it's the only thing you can do to help when they haven't yet awakened. She added that it was not the time to contact him, but I still did so with no luck. I need help; I am obsessed. It's such a difficult concept to get my head around; sometimes, I swear I'm conversing with him. I am, but it is his 5D, his higher self.

I'll explain what I understand about different dimensions.

Our 3D, 3rd dimension is the physical realm. It is what most of us operate from; it's an ego state. We live in a material world, separate from one another, where we judge ourselves and others on how we look, the car we drive, where we live, what we do for work, how much money we have, etc. In this state, we perceive life to be a competition, a survival of the fittest. We see and feel everything, good or bad, from a state of fear. Joy and fulfilment come from outside sources.

The 4D, 4th dimension is one I don't know much about. I am no academic or Spiritual Guru. I am the first to admit I can act daft at times, but my heart is always in the right place, so please excuse my inability to offer too much insight into this realm. I understand it's the intellectual realm or the gateway to the 5th. It's the realm where you start to question everything around you. We no longer take everything at face value; and are beginning to understand there is more to life than what meets the eye. We question everything we have ever known to be true and realise that our lives are what we make them; our energy creates our reality. The more we move away from 3D, the better and easier our lives become, and our desire for progress grows.

Our 5D, 5th dimension is the Spiritual realm. The 5D state is pure bliss. Life is wonderful; we realise we are all connected; we don't see people; we see Souls and are one with the Universe. We remember who we really are. We live life in a state of pure love. There is no competition, good or bad; it's just life, and we see everything with heightened awareness. Life flows freely and easily. Joy and fulfilment are found within. We naturally align with others on the same frequency and spread love everywhere. It takes courage and inner work to reach this dimension. If we all lived in a 5D state, there would be peace on Earth.

I believe all humans live in either the 3rd, 4th, or 5th dimension or a combination of all three. There are higher dimensions, but again, I do not understand; I have read that they are accessible to us after we have left our physical bodies.

Love, Michelle Ashton

Tuesday, 2nd May 2023

Dear Journal,

At my hairdressing salon today, I coloured my hair darker to stop dying it bright blonde. I made that decision along with removing my eyelash extensions. It's a hilarious thought to me now: sticking things on my eyelashes to make them thicker and longer and dying my hair to a colour that is, quite noticeably, not my natural hair. What was I thinking?

When I returned home from Paddington, I lay on my bed, looked at myself strangely in the mirror, and said, Michelle, in a deep voice. I scared myself and was shocked that my hair had changed. WTF. I knew I had gone to the hairdresser. If anyone saw that, they would call the ambulance and commit me. Hell, I am thinking of committing myself. This is even more clarification: this journey is the strangest thing.

Love, Michelle Ashton

Wednesday, 3rd May 2023

Dear Journal,

I'm not coping well today at all. I have massive anxiety, and everything is too much. I am unsure if it's my energy or if I am picking up from Adonis. Is he beginning to experience a dark night of the Soul? I am not sure what is going on: I can't cope, I cry, I drink wine, still sobbing, I run a bath. I get in the tub and shed some more tears. At this point on the journey, I have cried every day; I miss him so much.

- The dark night of the soul is a purification of the spirit. It is an excruciating experience akin to death and rebirth. This state can be triggered by a deeply painful period in one's life, such as the breakdown of a marriage or the loss of a loved one. I believe separation can initiate the dark night of the Soul during the Twin Flame journey.

Love, Michelle Ashton

Friday, 5th May 2023

Dear Journal,

I am Divinely supported; I know it. I read that Reiki helps with healing on the Twin Flame journey. I have previously had Reiki with some incredible practitioners over the years but was guided to a healer in Galston, NSW, over an hour from my home in Arncliffe. I have no idea what makes this Reiki healer so special, but today is my first appointment, and I'm about to find out.

I finally arrived home after being in the car for over 2 hours for my 90-minute appointment. I can barely find the words to explain this woman's craft. It's kind of a combination of holistic counselling and Reiki energy healing. Dani Divine Love is a Twin Flame and a gift from God, a living Angel. My Reiki Angel is the most intuitive, nurturing, compassionate healer with hands that can only be described as Divine talent. It was worth all the driving. This beautiful Soul explained she offers distance healing, but I would drive to Melbourne to be in this woman's company. This is the hardest thing I have been through in my entire life; I need all the healing I can get.

Love, Michelle Ashton

Sunday, 7th May 2023

Dear Journal,

I was guided to the Boho Luxe Market in Rozelle today. I may enjoy it, and taking my mind off Adonis for a moment would do me good. I arrive and think this is so me. Thank you, Divine, you know me so well. It is filled with sustainable products, boho fashion, crystals, sound healings, psychics and more. I came across a stall, The Healing Code Solution; ooh, you have my interest. I haven't experienced this modality in all my years. I need more information, what is this all about. The lovely woman Yenny explains that energy healing is performed via muscle testing, asking your subconscious mind questions and removing the trapped emotion from your energy field.

I'm in. We sit down; she does a little ritual, asking for permission. Absolutely, hell yes, let's proceed. Then Yenny asks if I want to work on something or leave it to my higher self. Please ask my higher self, who understands my needs better than I do. I sit there; Yenny does the rest; she uses a pendulum and an emotion chart and asks questions, though not to me directly. Some answers must not get a reaction as she moves on to the next question. I can tell when something arises as she goes further on her chart and back in years. I have a lot of childhood-trapped emotions. This does not surprise me in the slightest. Just before the session ends, Yenny clears all the trapped emotions and asks my higher self how long it will take to integrate. I am told that it will take seven days. I should start to feel a little lighter in a week. Though more than one session is needed for further healing, one will make a difference. We will see, hey. I will try anything to feel better. I can hardly function; I feel like a part of me is missing, and the only thing that I want and need to make me feel whole and take my pain away wants nothing to do with me. I did have a nice time today, but not for a minute did I stop thinking about him; it's hard to carry on conversations when all I can think about is Adonis.

Love, Michelle Ashton

Monday, 8th May 2023

Dear Journal,

I had another appointment with the Twin Flame reader today, but I'm still sceptical. I know she confirmed, and I sensed his presence in past life regression, but maybe he is a Soulmate. I keep researching; there is no denying all the symptoms match. I learned that there are similarities between a catalyst and a Twin Flame. Is that it? Is Adonis a catalyst? I also read that it is a normal part of the journey to doubt such an unusual phenomenon. The whole thing is mind-boggling; I don't know what to believe. I guess I won't know the answer until we talk one day.

The reader checks into his energy and reveals that he is in love with a Karmic partner, although they are not together. Not only are they a Karmic, but a narcissistic cheater, too. Gosh, poor Adonis, who is she talking about? I know how hard it is to break a trauma bond.

My heart breaks for him. Unfortunately, I know personally about both. I lived with a narcissist for 15 years. He controlled everything, including having a camera inside our Rose Bay home that backed up to his computer, watching my every move. All assets were in his name, and I had no access to his funds. He handled all the finances and paid the household bills. We had separate bank accounts, and he would give me some money each month and a credit card with a meagre limit for medical and household expenses only. If I had done something he wasn't happy about, he wouldn't pay the credit card; it would decline at the registers, which was very embarrassing at my age. When I complained, he would say he just forgot. Meanwhile, he had a Black Amex card with no limit, literally none; many times, he would purchase his expensive sports cars on the card to earn points, while I had a card that would sometimes decline for $150.00 at my doctor's surgery in Double Bay.

However, I was taken on luxurious holidays. He wasn't roughing it and bought me extravagant presents for my birthday. Even then, it wasn't about me; most years, he would pick a huge fight, and I would be in tears. I started to dread my birthdays. We had the most significant fight one year; I didn't open my present until two days later. I went for an MRI alone and was told to immediately return to my superhuman doctor, Michael Biggs, who broke the news. I had a brain tumour in my cerebellum and was to be admitted to hospital the very same day. I might die, so I may as well see my birthday present. I honestly believe the excessively expensive presents were for others, him showing off what he could afford, and for other men to be warned off. They would take one look at all the jewellery and think she's too expensive. I was also criticised for everything; I couldn't do anything right. Even the way I spoke was wrong in his eyes; I was given elocution CDs. Anyone in an emotionally abusive relationship understands how they manipulate and make you believe they only want the best for you. You completely lose yourself, eventually give up and do everything they want and how he or she would like things done, anything to keep the peace.

Cheaters, well, I have experience in that too, lucky me. It's Soul-destroying; your self-worth goes to shit, and you think somehow it's your fault. What's wrong with me? If only I had done this or not done that, or looked like this or had that, etc. You want to know everything, including everything about the other person. You compare yourself and think the other person is somehow better than you. You are so angry you want to revenge-cheat, and they say one in three people do. The cheater completely strips away your ability to trust, and you never look at people the same again. They take away your faith in humanity.

The reader also expresses that it's the Spiritual twin's duty to bring the Matrix twin to their awakening. The Matrix twin's psychic abilities lie dormant inside their DNA, waiting to be unlocked and eventually will surpass the Spiritual twin's abilities. I am told to stop contacting him to guide him to his awakening. Ha, easier said than done lady. This is a full-blown obsession. I cannot leave that man alone; I have no control. She explains that's why we must heal, learn to be whole and happy on our own, and have faith in God and the Universe. Ah, once again, this is the hardest thing I have gone through in my entire life. Talk about facing abandonment issues, fork!

- A Karmic relationship is an unhealthy past-life connection that is intense and emotionally charged. Karmic partners are drawn to each other on a Soul level, as they have unresolved issues. Depending on how much Karma needs to be balanced, these relationships can last weeks, months, years, or even decades. If we were to heal ourselves, we could clear the Karmic debt and not stay in these unhealthy relationships or even entertain them at all.

Love, Michelle Ashton

Wednesday, 10th May 2023

Dear Journal,

What is happening tonight? Is Adonis at a comedy event? Am I picking up on his energy, or is this just another part of the absolute madness that this journey brings? I can't stop laughing; it's not like something is a little amusing. Serious belly laughs. Something is hilarious. I am non-stop cracking up; I am not listening or watching anything; no one is here. There is nothing entertaining going on, except, of course, me laughing at nothing.

Love, Michelle Ashton

Sunday, 14th May 2023

Dear Journal,

Today is Mother's Day. I looked forward to taking my mum out for lunch and spending time with her, but she didn't want to go anywhere or have visitors. She and my uncle will visit my grandmother in the nursing home for a couple of hours; and adds she will be too exhausted afterwards. That's disappointing, but I am used to this kind of behaviour from my mother. I only see her a handful of times a year, and even then, it's challenging to arrange. She always complains about being tired or sick, or having to take care of the house, which my uncle had my grandmother sign over to him when she wasn't of a sound mind. My mother helped the process along by lying to the solicitor. By no means am I a fan of my grandmother; she was horrible to me as a child, but I feel for her; she is elderly and can't fend for herself. Once she signed her house over that she shared with my mum and uncle, she was sent off to the nursing home. I do believe it was time for her to go, but not in that way, without funding to have a choice of homes or her private medical cover that my uncle had cancelled on her. My mother and uncle don't work, and my uncle has been controlling her finances for years. All her money wasn't enough; he wanted her house, too. I can't fathom what kind of person could do this, and we are related. Exposing this truth is for Grandpa. May you now rest in peace.

Well, I have the day to myself then. There is a workshop at the Kadampa Buddhist Meditation Centre that I regularly attend. I love this centre. Everyone is so kind and friendly, from the Monks and Nuns to the staff and attendees. It is so refreshing; these are my kind of people. If only there were more people like this in the world, what a better place it would be. I hang off every word in these classes. Freedom of Forgiveness workshop, here I come.

Love, Michelle Ashton

Tuesday, 16th May 2023

Dear Journal,

I wanted an update, so I had another appointment with the Twin Flame reader today. I always wonder how Adonis is going. She checks in and says you might not want to hear this. He is going through a dark time; his kids and family are worried about him. He is so angry, fights with them, breaks things, and feels like he is losing control. This news breaks my heart; it sounds like he is going through a dark night of the Soul. I have such strong feelings for this beautiful man. I wish there were something I could do to help. I did send him an Instagram message trying to give him the heads up so he could understand a little. I didn't want him to be scared and blindsided like I was. I knew he wasn't aware of our connection, so I couldn't say much. I had to be obscure. I said something about being thrown into a Spiritual journey; that healing is tough but I hear it's worth the pain. Please, please believe me.

I pray every day for his journey not to be too hard or dark. I would give anything to be able to take some of his pain away. I have been through three myself; the pain is excruciating. In my two previous ones, I just thought I was depressed. My first was when Covid-19 hit Australia, and I had to close my wedding dress business. I had worked for years to make a name for myself in the Industry. Normal to feel depressed, right? My second was after my separation and divorce; the pain was so unbearable I started to lose clumps of hair. Again, it is expected to feel depressed. I had never considered anything Spiritual; it's so obvious now when I think of the changes that followed, like getting rid of expensive material possessions that no longer resonated. That should have made me consider it was ego-purging, but I was still in my 3D and looking for the most logical answer.

My third dark night of the Soul was brought on by Twin Flame separation. I went through this alone and told no one; I didn't want to be a burden. This one was hell. I have only journaled a fraction of the craziness and pain. Most days, getting through the day was an achievement, all whilst setting up my new business baby and crying, missing him, feeling like my Soul was being ripped out. I would pray to God, please take me now. I cannot endure anymore; I have nothing left to give. In saying that, I would go through a million more dark nights of the Soul if I could spare him from his and the pain associated. I wish I could trade places; I love him so much.

The reader can see the pain on my face and the compassion in my eyes, so she changes the subject and informs me he is spending a lot of time cooking. I thought he worked on the floor in the restaurant; perhaps he was cooking up a storm at home. I don't ask because she isn't aware of his job. I never divulge much information. First, I don't know much; second, it isn't my style. She says he is paranoid about our connection but not to worry. He is paranoid about a lot of things. Poor darling, someone has done a number on him. If only he trusted me enough to confide in me. I am his biggest cheerleader, bar none. She also adds he thinks I'm seeing someone as he feels my sexual energy; that is so funny; that's what I feel about him at times. Are we allowed to feel this to make us jealous? It seems a little cruel to me. I wish he knew I'm not seeing anyone or sharing my most sacred possession. I am in love and here waiting for him. Adonis, please put your skates on and hurry up. Every day without you feels like a lifetime.

Love, Michelle Ashton

Wednesday, 17th May 2023

Dear Journal,

Earlier, I had a phone call from a no-caller ID, as we all do many times, but this one was different. When I saw the missed call, I sensed it was him. I tried to call back, but it went straight to voicemail. Obsessively, I switched my phone to a private number, and it rang with no answer. There's my confirmation. I am blocked; he doesn't want to talk to me, but then I feel this kinky sexual energy. Is he with someone? Oh my, this is so forking tough.

Love, Michelle Ashton

Thursday, 18th May 2023

Dear Journal,

I'm so excited; I am booked into the pendulum workshop at the Mind Body Spirit Festival later today. Catch up after; bring it on!

I went along to the festival as I do almost every year. During this visit, I felt and absorbed so much more. I notice the shift, and I love it. The Mind Body Spirit Festival is pure perfection. Those are the only words to describe my feelings towards this incredible biannual expo. It's Australia's largest health and wellbeing event, and it's easy to see why. I once again came across Yenny from the Healing Code Solution.

My last session was 11 days ago; I feel lighter and believe it works. I'm in for another session. Yes, please, what a great way to start the festival day.

In between looking at all the beautiful stalls, I find the psychic reading room. There are many psychics to choose from, but I am guided towards Leon. I don't give him any information; I never divulge much to psychics. I want to see how good they are. Wow, he was phenomenal. It was one of the most beautiful readings I have ever had; it brought tears to my eyes. I felt so much love that I took a photo of the cards. It was heavenly. Thank you, Leon.

Next is an Aura picture. "Wow, there is so much orange colour." They then say, "Ooh, you're a creative one; what do you do for work?" "I'm launching a new wedding dress label, so I suppose yes, I am creative." That wasn't the only thing that caught their attention. They point to a flash of white light on my forehead. I ask "What's that?" "It's your 3rd eye; we take many photos and haven't seen one of those at this festival." It feels so nice to know that all the healing and meditation I am doing is taking effect.

I visit more wonderful stalls throughout the day, and I am so drawn to this gorgeous stall, Bespoke & Co Candles; it is filled with many beautiful things. I feel like a kid in a candy store. I decided on a charming cross and these stunning Angel wings. The absolutely lovely Soul Eleni explains that the Angel wings are hand-crafted by a renowned artist in Greece. Could they be any more special? I love them and promise to give them a good home. The Angel wings are heavy. "Can I please leave them here and pick them up after my upcoming workshop?" Eleni says "of course," and she also has a workshop coming up soon; "which one are you attending?" "I'm so excited, pendulum dowsing." "That's the workshop I am taking." I think about the Synchronicity; out of the hundreds of exhibitors, I was drawn to this stall moments before the workshop I had booked weeks ago. Spirit is reassuring me I am on the right path.

Eleni's workshop far exceeded my expectations. You can feel the love and energy she has for her classes. I am hooked; my pendulum now has pride of place in my home. What a wonderful day! If only I could have stopped thinking about Adonis and been fully present for all the beautiful Souls I had the pleasure of encountering.

Love, Michelle Ashton

Saturday, 20th May 2023

Dear Journal,

I tried to phone Adonis again on private number, but there was no answer. I think he should be awakened to our connection by now, so what the fork? He is either the rudest man on the planet or thinks he got a bad break. It would be nice to hear that he is aware. Geez, I'm not asking for his hand in marriage; I've been there and done that. I'm just asking for some common courtesy and decency. I'm getting frustrated not hearing anything, and honestly, it's bloody unfair. I have since sent him an Instagram message so he has concrete evidence from me; all I have is psychic confirmation and voices in my head. I should be the paranoid one.

Love, Michelle Ashton

Monday, 22ⁿᵈ May 2023

Dear Journal,

I had another beautiful healing session with Reiki Angel today. I showed her my Aura picture; she immediately noticed the green colour on my heart. Michelle, your heart chakra is open. I hadn't picked up on that before. Gosh, this woman is observant.

- Chakras are energy points in our body. There are seven main ones along our spine to the crown of the head. We want them to stay open; if they are blocked, symptoms relating to that particular chakra can arise. These can be either emotional or physical. It is said Twin Flames share a chakra system.

Love, Michelle Ashton

Wednesday, 24th May 2023

Dear Journal,

Tonight, I listened to a Twin Flames podcast. They were discussing Divine timing, making me think of Adonis and my failed marriages only a year apart. My marriage broke down in 2021, and his in 2022. They were always going to happen; it was Divine timing. Gosh, all that pain and heartbreak we both endured. If only we had hindsight, hey!

Suppose Divine timing is always at play; nothing I do or don't do will make one ounce of difference. I mean the healing, yes, we can't just sit around expecting to ascend magically without putting in the work. I am talking about contacting him and energetically chasing him. I cannot keep doing this to myself. It makes me so upset when I send a text that goes unanswered. I don't want to be sad. Logically, I understand this, but emotionally, the pull is too strong; I can't stop. I'm also cranky about checking his Instagram. I am a grown woman inflicting pain on myself. He was right when he said I don't respect his boundaries. I am a woman in love that knows no boundaries. I have shut my personal Instagram down; that should stop me. I love to look at business pages. Some of them are so interesting and informative, but when it comes to people's pages, most of them are ego-based anyway.

Love, Michelle Ashton

Thursday, 25th May 2023

Dear Journal,

Today, my mind is on Adonis, as always. I thought about how often I think of this beautiful man daily, and my conclusion is as much as I breathe. I wonder if he thinks of me loads or if it's just a chaser's role; I will never know until we speak freely. I also hope that one day, when we are by each other's side, he doesn't beat himself up about his behaviour. That was his role to play. Unfortunately, separation is inevitable unless both twins have done a lot of inner work before meeting; this work is integral to the Twin Flame journey. Both twins need to heal for a harmonious union. I have read on Quora about some exceptions, such as twins who can be ascended masters and reincarnate with a mission to help others. Others have noted that they managed to stay together and work through their healing journey. However, this is quite rare due to the intensity of the connection. Adonis had great intuition without knowing it in the 3D; he ended our fiery connection early on. It was a blessing I wasn't more attached. I can't fathom how much harder it would have been if we had spent real time together. Gosh, he is the most beautiful man on the planet. Even with the inevitable pain, he instinctively didn't make it harder or more complicated than he had to. My six-foot-five, Adonis, has a heart of gold.

Love, Michelle Ashton

Friday, 26th May 2023

Dear Journal,

I want to tell my brother about my Twin Flame journey. I love him so much; having this huge secret and not confiding in him is hard. I cannot take the chance of him getting smashed and telling one of his mates. I trust my brother when he is straight; you can't trust anyone 100% when they are high. Everyone divulges more than they would if they were sober. I have been around people taking drugs countless times in 30 years, listening to people discussing their problems and trauma and quite often hearing the same conversations over and over. Watching people bond over shared similar traumatic experiences. You can only imagine how useful the advice is coming from someone as high and forked up as you are. Seriously?

And yep, you heard that right: 30 years of taking drugs. The first time I took drugs, I was 16. My teenage boyfriend gave me a line of speed; I am now 47, so actually, that was 31 years ago. It's not something I am proud of in the slightest; when I say I have been around people taking drugs countless times, it would be in the thousands, so unfortunately, I know what I am talking about. When people take drugs, they talk shit. I can't risk telling Seb how much I love Adonis; the price is too high. It's an energy thing. If I am chasing, he will run further away. It's the push and pull dynamic of the Twin Flame journey. This separation is killing me. Seb would never hurt me intentionally; he could never grasp the implications. No one could unless you're a Twin Flame chaser; then you know exactly what I am talking about. It's pure hell, so I have to keep this massive secret from Seb, and Spiritual stuff will have to suffice for now. I pray this no-contact ends soon; I would love to hear from Adonis and be able to tell my bro. Not to mention, I might be able to sleep and get a massive energy boost to make it through the last ten hectic days before I launch my new business.

- The push-pull dynamic, also known as the runner-chaser, is easiest explained by the opposite of push is pull. The chaser is being pulled towards the runner while the runner is pushing the chaser away. Once both twins are healed, like magnets, they will attract each other with their perfectly balanced energies.

Love, Michelle Ashton

Saturday, 27th May 2023

Dear Journal,

I feel really down today; I cry this morning instead of dancing. I usually wake around five or six and jump straight out of bed, but not today. I woke up at five but still can't get up. It's now 10.15. I'm tired, my throat is so sore, I feel sick, and I'm just spent. This journey is so forking hard. I haven't heard one peep out of him, not a word; how much longer am I expected to put so much energy into something that may never happen? I love him so much, but he doesn't want a thing to do with me; how does one learn to live without their Twin Flame? Before this journey, you could have normal relationships. You may not have been as happy with someone else, but you wouldn't know that.

This journey has made me much more empathetic to help people, and I am grateful for that. Like yesterday, with Freida, she is the most beautiful Soul I have the absolute pleasure of seeing every Friday. Freida is an NDIS (National Disability Insurance Scheme) participant with the provider that I work for. I love caring for her; we call our Fridays spent together our feel-good Fridays. It was the first time in a while that she was well enough to go to the Central Coast and see her mum. I have been working with her at home for the last few weeks, so it was a big day for her. We chatted the entire way there and back; we had so much fun. I love that this journey has enabled me to help more than I could previously, but I'm tired. I feel weak and alone. I miss Adonis, the man I barely know on a 3D level. I don't know how much longer I can keep being supportive of what? I normally keep putting one foot in front of the other, but today, I cannot. I must get up to do some work; there isn't anyone else, but instead, I lay here in my tears, almost paralysed. I will pray again this morning that he finds the courage to make contact.

I have just logged back into my journal notes, and it's 11.30. I have lay in bed, crying for hours now. I have re-read every text message. I don't understand; for the most part, we get along effortlessly, and then, out of nowhere, he flips a switch. I'm making it so much worse for myself. Unless you're a Twin Flame chaser, you would have no idea the obsession that takes over. I will try to dry my eyes, put on my morning meditation, and then music to have a dance. I need to get myself out of this slump and try to forget the words from a text message he sent. It keeps repeating in my head: *I'm just not into you that way.* I must be a masochist; why else would I read that over and over again?

I still haven't gotten up. It's now 1.45; I don't have time to feel sorry for myself. How the fork am I supposed to do this? I keep setting myself up for rejection and pain. I have been so vulnerable with him; he hasn't given me anything in return. He couldn't give two shits. I know I'm supposed to send him love and good vibes, but I can't help but feel a little angry with this whole situation. I'm getting up now. I'm stronger than this; I must keep reminding myself of that. This is a pain like no other; it's not like the heartbreak I have experienced. Even just recently, all the shit I went through with Ian after 15 years together. Adonis and I spent no time together, and the pain is worse; it's like your Soul is being ripped out. I wonder if I can work on Valium? I have an alternative that the doctor gave me whilst going through my divorce. You can still concentrate and be alert. I'll take those to get through until my launch.

This afternoon and this evening was a little more relaxed. I realised that I needed to show myself some kindness, no matter how much work I had on my plate. I accomplished some work, practised yoga, had a few glasses of wine later, and indulged in a lot of chocolate.

I'm about to go to bed, but not before I check Adonis' focus status. Is he safe in bed? It's so stupid but comforting; I have completely lost it; it is forking ridiculous. I need to get a grip.

Love, Michelle Ashton

Sunday, 28th May 2023

Dear Journal,

I'm feeling calmer today; I'm unsure if yesterday was his or my energy. Unless you're a Twin Flame, you never have to question how you feel. I'm in a strange place, trying to decipher if my feelings are my own.

The weirdest thing just happened. Everything about this journey is bizarre, but how's this? Like every day, I'm hoping, wishing, and praying for him to make contact, but today, it's more than most. Then my phone makes his text chime. I froze, and I think I stopped breathing. I look at my phone, it's another friend. What is going on? Adonis is the only contact I have designated with that sound. I double-checked, and yes, I am right. My friend has the same text tone as my other friends. The Divine is magical, the synchronicity. That reminds me; I have been seeing number synchronicity for a while now.

- Number synchronicity is from the Spiritual realm, also known as Angel numbers. They are seen as Divine guidance; it's one way the Universe tries to communicate with us. It is a repetitive sequence of numbers that gives us advice and support.

Love, Michelle Ashton

Monday, 29th May 2023

Dear Journal,

I was in a good mood today, and then I had my beautiful Buddhist class tonight, which added peace to my demeanour. Unfortunately, it didn't last. After the class, I decided to check in with Adonis. I always send messages, hoping he has unblocked and stopped ignoring me. Another text goes unanswered. Why do I keep doing this to myself?

Love, Michelle Ashton

Tuesday, 30th May 2023

Dear Journal,

Another day, another text to Adonis, here goes.

This is another text that will most likely never see the light of day. I honestly don't know how to deal with this situation anymore or what my next steps should be. I can't live like this. I have One Kiss that I have worked so bloody hard for coming to life next

Tuesday. I have spent months finding it really difficult; there are no words to explain how hard it has been to work and try to be creative whilst not getting much sleep, not eating well, crying, going totally batshit crazy and longing for you to text me even to say hi to give me a little energy boost to make it over the line, but no nothing.

I feel so alone in this. I have always tried to help you by giving you a heads-up as much as I could without freaking you out before you understood and had time to process it. I am also trying to help you in ways you don't know by doing extra healing and trying to keep my vibe high. I had hoped by now you would unblock me. I don't understand and want to. I need something, not crickets. I don't know what else to say. It's making me feel like you regret ever locking eyes with me, which is beyond sad, but If that's how you feel, I am a compassionate person. I have so much love and respect for you that I will deal with it, but please show me some respect back. Crickets don't suffice x

Again, it went unanswered; maybe he has a girlfriend and is trying to move on. I've shed so many tears on this journey. I have to focus. I wish he would give me some clarification. I only have days left to complete so much work. I honestly feel like It's just not fair. Why does it feel like the runner holds all the cards, and chasers must wait? Fork this shit.

Love, Michelle Ashton

Wednesday, 31st May 2023

Dear Journal,

It's been one hundred sixteen days since I've seen his beautiful face and one hundred and eight days since he blocked me, but who's counting? I cannot allow myself to live like this; I will end up in a mental institution. It is so hard to let go when you know how perfect you are for each other. He is the only one with whom I can see a future. I can't believe he has opened my heart to love again. After everything I have been through, I never thought I would see the day. I will love him forever, but I need to work out how to deal with this shared energy and be happy with someone else. How does one move on from a perfect person? I have no idea. I can't put my life on hold for someone who shows me nothing in return. I have been so vulnerable and sent so many messages, each one unanswered. It's time to try to live life again. I believe in God and the Universe but also in free will. This is so sad. I have had visions of us laughing together. He feels like my home. I know I will still receive God's love and blessings; he sees all and will know I have done everything possible to revive this connection.

Love, Michelle Ashton

Thursday, 1st June 2023

Dear Journal,

This is a random entry, just another day on this crazy journey. I want to ask Adonis one day if he likes Mayer Hawthorne. I fancied listening to different music than I usually play, and his name popped into my head. I found him on Spotify and loved his songs. I had never heard of him before and wondered where the thought came from, and yes, again, I sent another text even though I said I wouldn't. I seriously need to stop this; it's Soul-destroying.

Love, Michelle Ashton

Friday, 2nd June 2023

Dear Journal,

I went to Galston after work today. I always love my sessions with Reiki Angel. I felt peaceful, and then disrupted my mood by sending another text. This is a daily occurrence, sometimes even more than once a day. I must get hold of this obsession; it's taking over my life.

It's sad that we cant talk, Im so excited & I wish I could share with you. Just getting all my stuff together to go live on Tuesday, finally

Hope you're doing well? Really mean that x

Love, Michelle Ashton

Saturday, 3rd June 2023

Dear Journal,

I forgot to mention that along the way, somewhere, I'm not sure when it started; It feels like forever. Salma calls him Adonis, too. I suppose it's because that's what I always call him. I'm not even sure if she remembers his real name. If I ever get to introduce them one day, I'd have to say this is Adonis, ha.

Love, Michelle Ashton

Sunday, 4th June 2023

Dear Journal,

Today is five months since locking eyes with this beautiful man, and my life as I knew it changed forever. I tear up at the thought. I thought I was living authentically before, so laughable. My only regret is that I didn't start my Spiritual journey earlier; I could have saved myself a lot of pain and heartache. Each of us gets to decide our destiny, and the life I was living wouldn't have led me where I wanted to go.

I will always love Adonis for helping me see things clearly. I do thank God for bringing him into my life. I bet I'm the first girl he has ignored who has said that to him.

Love, Michelle Ashton

Monday, 5th June 2023

Dear Journal,

I'm obsessed with making sure Adonis is ok. I worry so much about this beautiful man. He doesn't reply to my text messages, so I had another booking with the Twin Flame reader to find out. I tell her how much I hope and pray he will reach out, trust me and let me in. I am assured most Twin Flame runners reach out soon after awakening. She can't t tell me what the Divine plan is; all twins have different journeys mapped out, but in her experience, this is usually the case. She advises me not to get my hopes up as they don't always seek union. They typically are what she refers to as check-ins. However, she can put my mind at rest and tell me he is all right, but he thinks I have moved on as he can't feel my energy anymore. I am also told this happens sometimes; you can go through periods where you don't feel each other. I think the Universe must have known I needed a break this last week.

Love, Michelle Ashton

Tuesday, 6th June 2023

Dear Journal,

After what felt like the most prolonged pregnancy in history, I finally gave birth to my business baby. I went live today. The amount of research, work, time, and money that has gone into this venture is simply indescribable. Not to mention all the tears and anguish that came with a couple of near-death experiences. All new businesses take a lot to get off the ground, but I had more roadblocks than most entrepreneurs. I had two lengthy Covid lockdowns, as well as all the supply chain issues, extra costs, and setbacks that came along with it. Massive financial constraints meant I had to do most of it alone. I did have some helpers along the way, especially one that, until recently, had been with me from the very start. I will never forget her love, and unwavering support, to keep believing in my vision when things looked so bleak; she is such a beautiful Soul, thank you Georgia.

I only used contractors when absolutely necessary, so for the most part, it was just me; that was a full-time job in itself, but I also had to work two other jobs simultaneously to help fund the start-up. One was working with NDIS participants and the other driving for Uber. Add to that a 15-year relationship breakdown, a consequential divorce, and spending the last six months living in crazy town. To say I am proud of myself is the understatement of the century. I am about to go to bed after a long day, and the one person I longed to hear congrats from, nothing, not a peep.

I would have loved to have shared this special moment with him.

This was my first Instagram post since July 7, 2020, when I announced we were taking a short break—a month shy of three years.

We are so proud to bring this collaboration to life for our beautiful brides. One Kiss x Savvy Brides lets you choose from a range of bodices, skirts, different fabrics and colours to create your perfect dress, at an affordable price point. Made lovingly in Australia.

We are a wholly online business, we have no stockists or retail stores, meaning the sizeable mark-ups you find with the majority of bridal labels aren't passed on to you.

Our purpose is to make a positive impact in everything we do: for our brides, our community and the world we live in. That's why we have partnered with I=Change to make a charitable donation on your behalf with every dream dress ordered. You choose where the donation goes, and you can even track your impact.

Become a One Kiss babe and know that together, we're making a difference.

www.onekiss.com

I can't take credit for the post. It was written by a friend who also happens to be one of the most talented copywriters. Thanks, Rach de Hossan. It's perfect; I love it.

Love, Michelle Ashton

Wednesday, 7th June 2023

Dear Journal,

I'm so excited. It's the little things. Today, I picked up my framed Universe cards. Let me rewind. A couple of weeks ago, I was in the middle of a massive cleanout and came across my beloved Universe cards by Gabrielle Bernstein. I bought these a few years back; they speak to me, and I adore them. This beautiful woman has it figured out. I love them so much that I decided they were too precious to sit in a box. I never take time to do anything creative for myself, so I decided fork it. I went to Officeworks for supplies and had fun laying the cards out. I dropped them at the framers and got the call today. They are ready, yay. They are perfect for my home; I will now remember to read them daily. I wanted to share this news with Adonis, so I sent another text below. I live in hope that one of these days, I will get a reply.

New night, new journal entry ha. I will never know if I get to show you one day! I was really happy to pick up my personal stuff today. I am always doing stuff for work and I found these the other week whilst cleaning out (my Universe cards) so decided to take some time for myself and put them on cardboard and I had them framed. I love them not sure why I am sharing this info in my journal entry but I feel like you would get it :-)

I pray, just like I do with every other text, that I get a reply. Now, just getting my bro to hang them on the wall will be a feat in itself.

Love, Michelle Ashton

Thursday, 8th June 2023

Dear Journal,

I'm not feeling well. I work myself into the ground whilst on this crazy journey. It's all too much; I need a break. I want to build this business up quickly and fork off to a desert island without phone reception. What bliss, it probably wouldn't be because I'd still miss Adonis, every moment of every day. How does one get over this? I don't know; I seriously think I can't see a way out of this. I cry so much writing this, but it's true: how does one move on from oneself? How is this possible? Please, God, give me the answers; please help me; I'm struggling here.

Love, Michelle Ashton

Friday, 9th June 2023

Dear Journal,

I'm on a roll today. I started this afternoon by trying to call Adonis from my phone, but I'm still blocked. Next up, my work phone that's blocked, too. Now, I set my phone to private number, which goes to voicemail after two rings. I'm pissed. He has shown me no respect throughout this journey; he isn't the only one going through stuff; it's pretty selfish really. I texted him; it was the meanest I have ever been to this beautiful man. Does he think he can swagger on his back when he is good and ready? Fork this shit. I'm strong; I'll have to learn to live with his energy from now on, a new way of life, hey!

I have been nothing but nice to you for months & months & you just continue to have zero contact with me, not fair one bit, that's the least I can say. I wish the roles were reversed & you could feel how it feels!

It's been a few hours, and I get no reply, just like all the other text messages. I have had a couple of Friday evening vinos, and I've really got the shits now. I don't care if he is my Twin Flame; he is mean. I changed his name on my phone from Adonis to Mean Man and sent him the screenshot; I hope he sees that text message. He has hurt me so badly and, from what I can see, has zero remorse. I'm honestly in disbelief someone could act that way to another person, let alone the other half of their Soul.

Once again, I'm so upset and can hardly see through my tears. He doesn't give two shits; that's not the kind of person I want in my life. How the fork is he, my Twin Flame? I honestly can't understand; we are nothing alike in this instance. I couldn't hurt anyone, even someone I'm not fond of. Is he really that cruel, or just broken? What do they say hurt people, hurt people? I wonder what God's plan was. Why? Why put me through more hell? Haven't I suffered enough in my life? A forked-up childhood, forked-up teenage years, boyfriends that cheated on me, a violent one, a narcissistic, cruel ex-husband. Brain surgery, many other ailments, and always having to work my absolute arse off. I don't get it. When is it Michelle's turn to be happy, have fun, feel free, enjoy life, and be truly loved? When God, when? I pray it's soon.

Love, Michelle Ashton

Saturday, 10th June 2023

Dear Journal,

This morning, I woke up with determination. It is a blessing to be on this journey. Just because my Twin Flame is obnoxious, it isn't going to stop me from living my best life and helping people and the planet. I will continue to heal and try to stop losing my mind over him. Step one, I will not allow myself to check his focus status every night. This obsession with making sure he is safe and the tiniest little bit of feeling connected to him in some way has to stop.

<u>My healing helpers</u>
Having inspirational quotes and gentle reminders around my home
Practising positivity, kindness and gratitude
Self-love and self-care practices
Twice daily prayers and meditation
Eating a healthier diet, no more fast food
Spending more time outdoors
Exercising
Weekly Buddhist classes and monthly workshops
Chakra healing music
Yoga classes and workshops
I have a motivation app on my phone that sends messages 8 x per day
Listening to motivational podcasts
Past life regression
Healing code sessions
And my favourite, Reiki and holistic counselling sessions

I don't have a coach. I have read that it helps, but I don't have the time or the money. Anyhow, I feel really guided since tapping into my higher self; I am always guided in the right direction. It feels nice for once in my life to know that I am always being taken care of. Thank you, guides. I am so grateful; there are simply no words to describe my deep gratitude. Gabrielle Bernstein is correct; the Universe has your back.

Love, Michelle Ashton

Tuesday, 13th June 2023

Dear Journal,

I had a healing session with the beautiful festival healer, and I'm sad; this can happen after healing sessions. You don't always feel the benefits immediately. Sometimes, you need to work through the shadow and feel the pain. Whenever I think I'm at a place where I have turned a corner, something else comes up. I've had it: Universe, do whatever you want with me. I have surrendered to your outcome. I know you always want the best for me, but can I please have one request? Could you make it quicker? This healing bit isn't fun in the slightest. I am booking my Reiki sessions every few weeks on a Saturday afternoon, much smarter; this was dumb. It's a Tuesday, and I can't concentrate; I cry. This is so hard; I have no choice but to push through. Gosh, I hope it's not as bad for him. I don't see how it can't be; healing isn't easy. At least he knows I would be there for him; I don't have that. I feel so alone in this; at times, I feel like checking out to make the pain stop.

I sent yet another text. I never thought something like this would even enter my brain, let alone come out in a text to him.

I swore under no circumstances would I EVER contact you again without you contacting me first. I put all your texts into a different part of my phone so I could stop reading them. I can't help myself why the fork is everything your way, I have zero idea why I signed up for this & why did I have to go first. it's really forking hard, there is not one thing in the world you could say to me that would make me look or treat you any different than how I feel so I do not understand why you couldn't just touch base like any kind person & give me one tiny little bit of kindness & support. It's really unfair & I've completely had it, here's one more text for you that you or I would never think that would come out of my thoughts/ phone text or whatever here it is
FORK YOU!!!

- In healing terms, shadows are traumas, resentments, and fears sometimes hidden by our unconscious mind. We repress these wounds due to shame, terror or guilt, and they emerge as destructive behaviours—either harm to others or harm to oneself, such as eating disorders, alcoholism, drug taking, promiscuity, the list could go on and on. Our ego seeks validation for holding on to these shadows in ways such as telling ourselves a story to justify our destructive behaviour or hanging in a crowd where our behaviour is the norm. Well, if everyone else is doing it, it must be ok. Everyone else you know is doing it because our Souls naturally align with others vibrating on the same frequency.

To emphasise my point, the bottom line is you want to change your life, change your vibration. It is that simple, no joke. How do we do this? Love was believed to be the highest frequency leaving the human body, but we now understand its authenticity, so that's a good starting point.

Be authentic, and give others the space to do that, too. We don't have to run with the crowd, and whoever said beauty is on the inside couldn't be more correct. I am not suggesting we abandon rules, our friends or the things that make us feel beautiful or handsome. Just ask yourself, does this feel authentic to me? Does it align with my morals and values, not those of a partner, your peers, society, or a celebrity we admire? Basically, live our truth, and stand up for one's beliefs.

Following authenticity is love. Many of us find it easier to love others than ourselves. Truly loving oneself means having the courage to heal from the pain, traumas, fears, and wounds that hold us back from living our best lives. We need to stop making excuses: I'm not addicted, it's not my fault, it runs in the family, it's not a problem. I didn't have the proper education, upbringing or come from money; this and that happened to me; it's the cards I was dealt, etc. It's honestly incredible the bullshit that your ego will come up with to try to hold onto addictions or justify your reasons for not being able to go after the life you truly want. I believe having a colourful past or anything else we feel holds us back, such as poverty or, on the other end of the spectrum, living in the shadow of very successful parents, can give you even more determination to succeed. Those two extremes, wealth and poverty, have different challenges. Who are we to judge which is easier? I've heard poor people say, what problems do they have? Those people have money. How dismissive. We must stop judging each other. We have no idea; we haven't walked a mile in each other's shoes. The grass is not always greener. Simply put, stop making excuses and bloom where you are planted.

I understand that healing appointments cost money, but plenty of healing methods don't cost a penny. If you need a helping hand, I can tell you it was the best investment I have ever made. We all seem to find the money for our gym memberships, beauty treatments, fast food, alcohol, cigarettes, drugs or whatever our vices are; heck, some of us even prioritise these over basic needs. I know I always found the money for drugs. I understand that some of us find it difficult to put food on the table and don't have a spare dollar, so start with kindness. Kindness is free. Kindness to yourself and others. Start practising kindness, which includes self-healing, and watch how magically your life begins to improve.

I also acknowledge that others in the world lack food or shelter and will not have the opportunity to read or hear about this book. So, I beg the rest of us to join the movement to raise our vibration and watch our lives flourish while benefiting humanity and the planet.

Please don't be scared off by my harrowing healing journey. You will never be shown what you aren't ready to deal or couldn't cope with. Your Soul knows exactly what you can handle, even though, at times, it doesn't feel like it. Don't get me wrong, healing is never fun or easy, but you can move at a slower pace. I was determined to heal my wounds as quickly as possible. Reiki Angel commented that she had never seen someone move so fast in their journey. I just knew what I had to do, like driving home on autopilot. I didn't realise at the time I had a mission to fulfil.

The self-healing techniques that I found helpful

- Practising positivity, kindness and gratitude
- Journaling- It doesn't have to be a work of art; write down thoughts and feelings
- Letting myself feel the pain, instead of sweeping it under the rug (on many occasions, I would drive to the middle of nowhere and scream at the top of my lungs; it feels so good to let it out that goes for tears too)
- Being outdoors
- Eating a healthier diet
- Exercising
- Prioritising sleep
- Meditating
- Yoga
- Self-care practices like taking a bath or anything else that brings you joy that isn't destructive to your life.
- Good, clean, fun. I love spending time with my niece and nephew; laughter is the best medicine.

So much love, Michelle Ashton

Wednesday, 14th June 2023

Dear Journal,

I have been less than loving the last few days. I wonder if he has picked up on my energy. I'm just tired; it's so forking hard. I love him and always will. He will always be my Adonis.

Love Michelle Ashton

Thursday, 15th June 2023

Dear Journal,

Tonight, I decided to be kinder to myself. Instead of drinking wine and eating chocolate, I had a sauna and listened to a podcast. It's not the first time I have heard about this mirror exercise. I will ask Reiki Angel about it on Saturday. I will try anything; I am now so open to healing, and even though it's so hard, I am determined to make it to the other side.

- The mirror exercise is a Spiritual tool for self-transformation. Our external reality is only a reflection of our inner world.

Love, Michelle Ashton

Friday, 16th June 2023

Dear Journal,

I felt sexual energy last night; I don't know where it comes from; it's not mine that I know. I wonder if he was either intimate with someone, asleep and dreaming, or you know what, ha. This type of energy coming from your Twin Flame is hard to bear. My brother told me he had a girl keeping his bed warm, so to speak, in a flash after me, but that was the start of this journey. It wasn't as hard to handle. Heck, I've even thought I would like to join Spiritual Singles to meet a match, but at this point in the journey, I couldn't even consider it. Adonis is the only man for me. He is beautiful inside and out, perfect actually. The most handsome man I have ever laid eyes on.

Love, Michelle Ashton

Saturday, 17th June 2023

Dear Journal,

I'm in a good mood today, which is a strange feeling of late. I wonder if Adonis is happy, and we are mirroring each other. I won't know until I see his beautiful face.

Love, Michelle Ashton

Sunday, 18th June 2023

Dear Journal,

I'm so sick of this roller coaster. I felt good all day yesterday and again today until 4.45 pm. I couldn't hold my tears back even to make it upstairs to my apartment. The people in my building must think I am the biggest crybaby. I have no idea how anyone survives this journey. I refuse to let this beat me. I don't even know if this is my sad energy. I couldn't help but worry about him, so I texted to ask if he was okay. He doesn't seem to care about my well-being; is it just a chaser thing?

Love, Michelle Ashton

Monday, 19th June 2023

Dear Journal,

I have been awake since 4.30 am and the sleep I did manage to get was very restless. I need to balance these energies. I can't live and work without sleep; today is going to be a killer. I have no idea how surgeons could go through this and get up to go and operate; I can hardly operate my brain.

This is so off-topic, but I have to add that tonight, after I got home from my beautiful Buddhist class, I realised how tight my jeans are getting. I can't remember the last time I went to the gym. The last time, I didn't consume so much food just for some energy. Then I turn to my face; the bags are enormous; I haven't slept well in months. I don't even look like myself anymore. Quite frankly, I look like shit, and I feel like shit.

Love, Michelle Ashton

Tuesday, 20th June 2023

Dear Journal,

Something has changed; I can feel it. I almost cry writing this; to feel he is happy makes me so happy, so I'm in a particularly good mood. There is just one strange thing that has developed. I have gone off meat and chicken. The thought of a steak grosses me out no end, and then I tried to eat a chicken schnitzel sandwich this morning; it was so gross. I picked all the chicken off and ate the avocado. What's going on with me? I wonder if this vego thing will stick. I did this for some time in my 20s for health, and I hated feeling like a nuisance when I went for dinner at friends' houses, but this is different. I feel so much compassion; to think an animal has to lose its life so that we can stuff our faces is absolutely disgraceful.

Love, Michelle Ashton

Wednesday, 21st June 2023

Dear Journal,

This morning, I had a session with a psychic; I never give away much. She told me a friend of my brothers likes me, but they think there might be an issue with him. Also, this man has children and is a very good dad. Mmm, is she talking about Adonis? He has kids, and I bet he is a good dad. She adds that he has someone into him at a swimming group, and they used to hang out, if you know what I mean, but he is no longer interested. I know Adonis likes to swim, so it sounds like him. I understand no one can have what we have, but it still hurts to hear about other women.

Later this afternoon, I picked up lots of veils for work. Now, I can't use my kitchen or burn my eco-incense because it will make them smell. It's a minor problem in the scheme of things—first-world problems. I love my incense; it makes me happy, and I can't do it. I'm just feeling sorry for myself. I work so hard, and Adonis doesn't contact me. I want a break. This has been going on for months now. It's really starting to take its toll on me and my health. I don't know what each day will bring. I've had more panic attacks in the last few months than I have had in my entire life. It's all too much, and I don't tell anyone; I don't want them to worry, but between you and me, I'm struggling big time.

Love, Michelle Ashton

Thursday, 22nd June 2023

Dear Journal,

This morning, I was eating my cereal, and the bowl was in my left hand instead of on the table, as usual. I wouldn't normally do this, as I know there's a big chance the bowl would drop. I finished my cereal and burst into tears, happy tears. I was so proud that I pat myself on the back. I thought I had dealt with all the emotions from my brain surgery a long time ago. But no, I'm still crying; this wound is deep. I now know I need to feel the emotions to move past them. I have always stopped myself in the past because who wants to feel pain, right? I have pushed this under the rug for years. It's now 2023. My surgery was in late 2011. I didn't allow myself to feel the emotions; I just had to get on with it, learning to walk again and live with the new challenges I faced. I think about how lucky I am to be here; Adonis wouldn't have had a chance to find me in this lifetime.

Later in the evening, I ordered tofu and veggies from my local Thai restaurant. I noticed that I've been eating lots of vegan meals lately. I still can't stand the thought of eating an animal; eww, gross. While waiting for my meal, I casually talk to my bro. He tells me Noah texted him out of the blue last Sunday, after months of no contact, and he wanted to catch up to have a chat. Seb, it's now Thursday; you are hopeless with replying. I ask my bro to reply and to please smooth things over. It's very important, can you please do this for me. Seb says, "Of course, Shelly." Oh my gosh, I am so forking happy. YAY, Adonis is making some progress. I had the biggest smile; I stood out of my seat and jumped around!!!!!

Love, Michelle Ashton

Friday, 23rd June 2023

Dear Journal,

I woke up feeling confident in this connection. I am so grateful. Seriously, pinch me. How did I get so lucky? It's the most beautiful connection you could ever have. I've never experienced the love that I have for this beautiful man; it's unexplainable. There are no words; not often am I lost for words. We are so blessed to have found each other in this lifetime: Thank you, God, and thank you, Universe.

Love, Michelle Ashton

Saturday, 24th June 2023

Dear Journal,

I spoke to Seb, and he informed me that Noah replied; he said he was off to Thailand for a couple of weeks and would like to catch up when he gets back. I'm delighted for him; if his healing journey is anything like mine, a holiday is exactly what he needs. I hope he has a beautiful, relaxing time away. I've never felt this way, where I am so happy for someone else and care so much about their well-being. Don't get me wrong, I'm always genuinely happy for my family, loved ones, and even those I don't know. I'm the kind of person who smiles at the TV, but this is entirely on another level. The amount you truly want that person to be happy Is an unconditional love I have never felt before. I love this man so much, and to think I hardly know him. My feelings alone are proof enough of a past life connection.

Love, Michelle Ashton

Sunday, 25th June 2023

Dear Journal,

Salma and I were discussing Tony Robbins. I bought a ticket to Unleash the Power Within, his Sydney event, held later this year. It was expensive, I couldn't afford it, and I had no idea how to take the time off, but I booked it anyway. I thought this is an investment in your future, Michelle. Salma said she loved watching his documentary, I Am Not Your Guru and thought I would like it too. I watched it on my brother's Netflix, and Salma was right; I loved it. Tony was discussing mothers and fathers; he said his mum used to beat the shit out of him. I have such compassion, and at the same time, I'm totally in awe of this man. The courage and strength it would have taken to go from that life to where he is now. It got me thinking about my parents and younger years, and I started to cry. It's something I never like to discuss. I don't want people to look at people I love differently, so I keep it to myself, but now I know I need to voice it and feel it to heal it. So, Journal between you and me, here is a brief background of my life up until thirty years of age when I met my ex-husband Ian in late 2005.

I am the eldest of my parent's three children. I have a brother, four years and a sister six years younger than me. My brother and I have father unknown on our birth certificates, but we look and act more like Dad than our sister. I was born at 3.27 pm on the 24th of September 1975 in Bankstown Hospital, a south-west suburb of Sydney. I was given the name Michelle Anne Ashton. My brother and I weren't given Dad's surname until they were married a few years later. I'm unsure where we lived then; the earliest photos I recognise are from the granny flat behind my dad's father's house in Bass Hill, near where I was born. Between then and starting school, we moved to public housing in Airds, another south-west suburb of Sydney. It ranks as the number one spot with the most public housing in Sydney, which ¾ of the population lives in, and a large portion are on welfare, including my parents. I spent kindergarten at Briar Road Public School and made friends. My best friend was a sweet girl named Kathleen. I was happy. I was too young to understand that we were poor; it was just life, and mine didn't seem different from my classmates.

When I was six years old, my mum and dad divorced. Their marriage was very short-lived and I moved with my mother to Macquarie Fields; at the time, this area also ranked high as a disadvantaged area of Sydney. I started at the local school and was bullied by a group of 5 much older girls. I have no idea why they honed in on me, but I was scared to go to school. I remember hiding under a tree all day, pretending to be there until my mother caught me and sent me back. We were broken into in this house; they took everything, our TV, stereo and other cherished items, also clothes, toys and even meat from the freezer. I was scared in this house. I hated my school; my dad had already shacked up with my new step-mother. My mother wasn't happy; she was single, on welfare and in unsafe public housing with three young children. I hated home life and school life, so at only six years old, I hated my entire life.

Things didn't get much better in the years following; I lost count of how many times we moved. A few years later, my mum started dating my aunt's long-term partner, my cousin's stepfather. It was weird that she was dating a man we used to call uncle, and it meant another move, but she was happy again. One night, my brother and I heard noises from my mother's bedroom. We watched them having sex; we decided to copy them. We didn't know what we were doing, and neither of us were aroused; it was just two kids rubbing their bits on each other. I have never told anyone that; I haven't even discussed this with my brother in all these years. I don't even know if he remembers. I felt so guilty when Mum lost it and sent him to his father's house to live. We had both watched her, but she didn't send me; he was mischievous and hyperactive, so naughty, in fact, that one day, he set the inside of a car on fire. She could have just said she couldn't cope instead of making us both feel guilty; we were just kids. I don't know the details, but Mum had an abortion, and her boyfriend was gone; she told me they broke up because I misbehaved, and he was going to smack me. She said to me no one will lay a hand on my children. So, selfless. I felt guilty because she was single and unhappy. If this was the reason she broke up, why tell me? Let's fast-forward to my first year of high school.

I started at James Meehan High in Macquarie Fields while living in public housing. I had just settled in; I don't know if I was there for a month. It seemed like it was just in a blink when Mum said we were moving. This time, it was to a caravan in my grandparents' backyard in Chester Hill, a suburb of Canterbury Bankstown, not far from where I was born. The three of us, my mum, my sister, and I, lived in a caravan without facilities; we had to go inside for meals, the shower and the toilet. If we needed to pee in the evenings, we had to use a potty that was emptied each morning. I attended Sefton High School and made friends, but they were not allowed to come over; these were my grandmother's rules. This was just one rule of many; others consisted of dinner at 4.30 pm. One quick shower per day, at a time chosen by her, and you could have a slightly longer shower once weekly to wash your hair. I could go on and on; this was a house of rules.

I fought with my grandmother; we even went to counselling until she stormed out of the session when the counsellor said something she didn't like. I hated it there, but I did love my grandfather; he was always so good to me. He used to sneak me treats, and we would hang out in his TV room and watch the cricket. I was so grateful that I had him, but Nan ran the house, and everyone feared her. She used to bad mouth my dad all the time, who I loved very much, and it hurt to listen to her barrage. One day, I had enough and stood up for him; I couldn't hear it any longer. I then said I wanted to go and live with Dad. She picked up the beloved pink ghetto blaster she had given me as a present. I didn't have much, and I cherished it; she knew it and said well, you're not taking this with you, and smashed it to pieces in front of my face. I cried so hard; I was 12 years old. I feel sorry for Grandpa that he married her. He was an upstanding man, a police officer and an old-fashioned country boy. He wouldn't have dreamt of divorcing. He was the kindest man; I can only imagine what he had to endure. I can understand why he turned to alcohol.

Still, in my first year of high school, I move to Culburra, a south coast suburb of NSW, to live with my dad, stepmum, and brother. This is the story I tell myself of where I grew up and anyone else that asks. I loved being with my dad and brother. Even though Dad takes drugs and is an alcoholic, he is a loving and fun dad. I am not used to this; Mum is cold and unemotional. At Dad's, we spend time at the beach almost daily; we have fun, and he makes me laugh. We can use the facilities whenever we wish; this household has no set times. I'm allowed to watch movies and listen to music; I have my own bedroom, and I can have friends over. Is this what it's like to be a kid? It makes the hour-long journey on the school bus each way a piece of cake. Everything is going great, except I don't like my dad's friends. They scare me. One day, I walked into his bedroom; he had built the house himself but hadn't put doors on the rooms yet. I saw his friends shooting up; I was so scared I wet my pants. His friends don't always come over so that I can deal with, but my step-mother is always in my face. Every day, she finds something to be annoyed with me about. She has my name on a wooden spoon, and smacks me with it. I want to please her because I like it here, but nothing I do works. I feel like she doesn't like me, and then I understand. I overhear that she can't stand me as I remind her of my mother. After a short time, I'm shipped off back to where I came from. No wonder this is the story I tell myself; even with my dad's druggie friends and my step-mum hauling me over the coals every day, it was still the best couple of months of my entire childhood.

After I had moved out, my step-mother decided they were all moving interstate to Tasmania. I was so distraught, begging my dad not to leave. I was crying and pleading with him, "Please don't leave; I won't get to see you in the school holidays." He said, "I have to Sis," and they moved. This was my first heartbreak; I was abandoned by the man I loved. I couldn't understand why they had to move; my dad loved that house and being by the beach. Why couldn't he stand up to her? I am his daughter. He was supposed to protect me. There was no chance of living with them again or spending time with my dad and brother. Holidays were impossible; the costly flights were not within my reach. Even to this day, I have been to Tasmania once, and they have lived there for over 30 years. Dad has made two trips to Sydney, one just recently and one for my brain surgery. Mum didn't come to see me in the hospital, and she lives a 45-minute drive away. I wonder if she would have bothered to go to my funeral if I had died in the six-hour-long surgery.

I am back at the caravan in my grandparents' backyard under my grandmother's rule. Still, in my first year of high school, I returned to Sefton High and even under the harsh living conditions, I have something to be so grateful for. This time, I met my best friend Salma; we have this beautiful friendship that has survived the years. Salma is so special to me; she is such a kind and caring friend. She is bloody funny, and cracks me up like no other—the only person in my entire life who has never let me down. I am so grateful for her friendship; I only hope I am as good a friend to her.

Now, in year nine, we have moved into a flat, and there are just the three of us. I share a room with my sister; we have double bunks, but Mum has her own room, one less person to hear at night. I get to attend the same school this time and am so happy. I loved this school; I really enjoyed photography. I won a Sydney Morning Herald Newspaper competition, and I have my lovely photography teacher, Mr. Kline, to thank for it. This time, like many other occasions, he had paid the two dollars for me to be able to attend the excursion. I was told no, I couldn't go, we couldn't afford it. Mr Kline was such a kind man; he saw my potential. Thank you so much; I have never forgotten him and his kindness.

I'm old enough now to get a part time job. I start working at Kmart. Yay, I am earning my own money; even though I have to pay board, I can buy things. I met a girl who goes horse riding with friends on the weekends; she invited me along. That sounds fun; I go, and I'm not into horse riding; but there is a guy I'm interested in. I thought he was cool with his long hair; he was of legal age, had a car, drank, smoked, and seemed quite rebellious. We start dating, and at 14 years old, I lose my virginity. Even though it hurt so much, I feel like a woman now. We continue to have sex all the time; I feel like I've discovered the best thing since sliced bread. After a while, he becomes so controlling, wanting to know my every move. I decide to break it off with him. He asks one last favour: can I come to his house and say goodbye to his mum? They live in Mascot, an inner-south suburb of Sydney. Avoiding tolls, It's about a forty-five-minute drive away from our flat in Carramar, but that sounds like a fair request.

We walk into his house, and he throws me in his room and locks the door; he won't let me out, not even to use the bathroom. The things he is saying to me are so scary, and he is furious; I have never seen him like this, I'm bloody terrified. His mother comes to the door begging him to let me out. He tells her to mind her own business; I am so scared he might go through with his threats to kill me. I don't know how long I am here. It was light when we arrived, and now it's really dark; it must be late at night. Why is no one coming to find me? He leaves the house to get cigarettes out of his car, its parked on the street; the door is ajar. It's now or never. I bolt out and down the street as fast as I can, screaming help me, help me! He is chasing me; I have never run so fast, jumping fences and bashing on doors. No one is opening; what will he do to me now if he catches me? Finally, I bash on a girlfriend Heather's dad's house; kind Des hears me and opens the door to let me in. Phew, I'm safe, he called the police. I don't know what my ex-boyfriend said to them, but they returned and said they could only issue a restraining order. Are they serious? He is a madman. A temporary restraining order is placed immediately, but I must go to court and face him to receive a longer one. I never wanted to see him again as long as I lived. This is the one bit of extra support I have gotten from my mother over the years; she did come to court with me, as I was bloody petrified. The only good thing about having a relationship with this madman is I met a beautiful girlfriend, Heather; we became very close and would always hang out. I loved her and her family.

I put this behind me and started living my life again. I applied for a photography traineeship in the city of Sydney. I was interviewed, and got the gig. I'm now 14 and 9 months old and working full time. I loved not feeling reliant on anyone; this is freedom. Mum met another guy around the same time, and we moved again. It didn't bother me this time because I was always out. I had met my teenage boyfriend in an eastern suburb nightclub. I had used a girlfriend's birth certificate to get in; there were no photo ID's in those days. I was so in love, well, what I knew love to be at the time; he was just as crazy in love with me. We quickly became inseparable. His mum was so good to me; I absolutely loved her. She would cook for me most nights, and I would eat with her, his dad, and brothers. I felt part of a real family. They even took me out for their family dinners; I remember the first time I hadn't been to a proper restaurant before and didn't know what to order. I just copied what my boyfriend, the birthday boy, was having. Yes, thank you. I'll have the lobster, too. To this day, it cracks me up. I didn't even know what it was, let alone that it was the most expensive item on the menu.

My mum wasn't as accommodating with him, so we didn't spend much time at my house. One day, he dropped me back, and no one was home. We started making out, and by now, we were half undressed. We hear the door, grab our clothes, and hide in the laundry. Mum catches us, sends him home and gives me an earful. I try defending myself when her boyfriend walks in and screams at me to get out. Mum agreed with him. I am to leave; I have nowhere to go. I have already been abandoned by my father, now my mother. I went to my grandparents' house to ask if I could live with them; that's how desperate I was. My grandmother said no; I had only just recently turned 16 and had nowhere to live. I call my boyfriend in tears. He lives at home and shares a bedroom with his brother but is frantically trying to find somewhere suitable. He finds a room to rent in a police officer's flat in Maroubra near his house in the eastern suburbs of Sydney. I can move in tomorrow, perfect. I just need to find somewhere to stay tonight. A friend lets me sleep on her lounge room floor; she already has someone on her couch. At least I'm safe for the night.

16-year-olds don't earn much money, so the rent is quite expensive. It isn't easy, but my boyfriend is working and is very generous. He always takes me out and buys me things. We really enjoy each other's company; we are joined at the hip. He drinks a lot, but I am used to that with my dad and grandfather. We are so in love that we even discussed that when we are older, we will marry. Now, I have my own place; we have a lot of sex, so I am on birth control. Oh, fork, this is a big surprise! Oh my gosh, you guessed it. I'm bloody pregnant. My boyfriend wasn't happy about it, it wasn't my fault. It was not intentional, that's for sure; we were so young. I always thought we would have children when we were older, but not now; we were kids ourselves. I have wanted to be a mum from as young as I can remember. I used to do everything for my little brother Seb; I always wanted to feed and care for him like my baby. This is not in my plan, but I am here anyway. I didn't know how it could work, but I knew I wanted to be a mum one day, so I decided to keep the baby. We don't tell his parents; he thinks they will flip, they will find out eventually, but we figure we will work it out later. Things were not like they once were between us; we started to argue a lot. He used to drink and pick fights with others; he was an aggressive drunk but not ever towards me; he always doted on me, but now things had changed. He was so stressed, I was starting to show, and we still hadn't told his parents. We had no idea where we would live or how we could even care for ourselves, let alone a baby. One night, he was drinking, and we argued so much. I was so distressed that I cried myself to sleep that night. The next day, I awoke to blood. I went to the hospital; I had suffered a miscarriage.

If things weren't bad enough, the company I worked for no longer had use for a junior, so now I don't have a job, and until I can find another, I'm on welfare. The payments don't even come close to covering my expensive rent in the eastern suburbs. I have to move; I have no job and nowhere to live. Another girlfriend, lived with her mum in Mascot, and her dad lived alone in a two-bedroom apartment in the same suburb. I can stay with him. It was very short-lived; one night, he climbed into my bed whilst I was asleep. I awoke to an old man smelling like a brewery, touching my private parts. I asked him what the hell he was doing and to stop. He did listen, but I was asked to leave the next day. I never told a Soul; I didn't want my friend to think badly of her dad, so it is just another thing to add to my long list that I need to voice and feel to heal. So where to now? My girlfriend, Heather, had a family friend who owned a mechanic workshop in the industrial part of the airport suburb of Mascot. He had a room upstairs at the back of the workshop for himself with the facilities and another tiny little loft area on the side of the workshop that housed a single bed. You had to walk through the workshop to get to the stairs, and once inside, you had to duck into the tiny room and back through the workshop to use the facilities. I was just so grateful to have a roof over my head, even if I could bang my noggin on it. This man was kind.

The kind man had a younger girlfriend, she was older than me, but we knew each other as she was a friend of a friend. My boyfriend took me out to a nightclub in Mascot one night and started to cry; he kept saying how sorry he was. I'm worried. I've never seen him like this. What's wrong? What are you sorry for? He told me he had cheated on me, he was so sorry, it was a one-night stand, and he regrets it so much. He loves me, and it will never happen again. I can't believe what I'm hearing. I scream at him, with who? He doesn't want to tell me. I demand to know; I am so angry. He spills the beans, and the kind man who is letting me stay in his workshop, it's his girlfriend, and I saw her walk into this very nightclub; she is upstairs from us. Heather and I walk straight up to her and confront her. I am screaming at her. She apologised, and her defence was that she was jealous of me. Seriously? People have no idea of others' lives. I am livid; then I realise I am livid at the wrong person. Sure, she is a complete bitch for coming on to my boyfriend, but it takes two to tango. I am sad, I am angry, I feel so betrayed. I loved him so much that I wanted to marry him one day.

I forgive him, but I'm still so angry. You know previously how I said one in three people revenge cheat. I'm so ashamed to say I was the one in three, but I didn't just cheat once; mine turned into an affair. I am so sorry I used someone else to get back at my boyfriend. My affair guy genuinely liked me and wanted to introduce me to his family; that's when I realised how he felt, and I broke it off with him. I am so regretful; he didn't deserve that, and I can't apologise enough for my despicable behaviour. I felt so guilty, and I confessed everything to my boyfriend. We fought so much, but eventually, he forgave me. We are back together after both being unfaithful, but we keep fighting, blaming each other, breaking up, and getting back together. I am unsure how many times we did this, but in the end, we broke up for good. Between the both of us, we had ruined what had been a beautiful relationship.

I finally landed another job. Yay! It wasn't easy, given my lack of experience and education. I am so happy to be working again. I work in a taxi centre, giving students their street directory tests. I still don't get paid much, but I can move out of the workshop. A couple I became close with whilst dating my teenage boyfriend have a one-bedroom flat in Randwick, located in the eastern suburbs of Sydney. They are renting out their sunroom it doesn't have a door, but it's a lot better than where I have been staying, and it's a reasonable price. I have a single mattress on the floor, I can stand up straight in the room, and I don't have to walk through a dirty workshop. These digs are plush.

My boss at work asks me to come out for drinks with a group. We all go out; he buys the drinks, and everyone is drunk, including me. He decided we would go to another bar in Oxford Street in Surry Hills. We all walk in and take a spot downstairs. What is this place? It doesn't look like much fun to me. It's kind of like a shisha bar with private areas. He asks me to come upstairs. There are cushions everywhere; this is a bloody weird bar. He throws me down and licks all over my face, trying to get his tongue down my throat. I keep saying what are you doing? Get off me. One of the other employees comes upstairs in the nick of time; leave her alone. I run out shaking and go home. The next day, I went to work a little hungover, as if nothing happened. My boss apologised for his drunken behaviour. I really need this job, so I go about my work, thinking all is fine, but not long after, I am fired.

This time, I am desperate to find another job quick smart. I have no savings; I don't have anyone to fall back on. If I don't find something quick, I will be homeless. I don't have much experience or education, so it's really tough. I found a receptionist position in the local paper that advertises no experience necessary will train. I immediately called them, and they were able to interview me the same day. Wow, this is looking promising. I get all dressed up and go to the interview; it's dark in this office. The man explained what they do: it's an adult massage parlour. They need another receptionist ASAP, and another staff member will train me. I don't even know what an adult massage parlour is, but I can tell it looks seedy. Is this even legal? The money is good, so I decided not to ask questions. I start straight away; a lovely older lady trains me. She teaches me on the phone, how to fold towels and get the girls' rooms organised. I am ready for my first shift by myself. I am so nervous; most girls are lovely and helpful; they know what they are supposed to do and help me find my feet. The phones are terrifying; they have a standard spiel for each girl, but some men ask more questions. I got used to this, but not this call. The man on the other end asked if I was new and what I looked like; he hadn't heard me before. I say yes I'm new, ignore his other question and run through the girls working that shift. He is unsure who he wants to see, so he books the room for later in the afternoon.

The gentleman who calls himself Peter arrives for his afternoon booking. I take him into his room and start sending all the available girls through to introduce themselves. I return to the room to ask who he wants to see; he says you. Sorry, I only work reception. He turns on the charms and doesn't stop trying to convince me. He is offering me more and more money to massage me and adds that I don't have to touch him. The money is almost as much as I make in a week, just for 30 minutes. The boss comes in to see what's happening; they seem to know each other well. Peter explains, and the boss suggests getting one of the girls to handle the phones for half an hour. Oh, fork, here goes. I take the money and undress. I have never been so nervous; I feel sick. Peter is lovely and tries his hardest to calm my nerves; he says all the right things. He is very charming. I lay face down on the massage bed. He starts massaging my naked body; this 30 minutes is going to feel like a week. It's time to turn over; I think I'm going to throw up. I have only been naked in front of a couple of guys before. He is massaging me, touching my breasts, and now his hands are moving towards my private bits. He is very gentle, but I feel sick. The time is up; thank goodness I can breathe again. I managed to pull myself together enough to finish my reception duties.

The day is over, and I have the house to myself. My flatmates are away for a few days, so the timing couldn't be more perfect. I need not talk to anyone tonight. I get home, pour myself a stiff drink, and sit on the couch. I start thinking about today's events. This is not crying; this is wailing. I feel like I have sold my Soul. I take some prescription medication to calm me, but it's not working. I take more and more. Fork it. I decided to finish the bottle of meds. I don't want to be here anymore. This year, I have been kicked out of home, had no place to live on more than one occasion, fallen pregnant, miscarried, been unemployed, had my friend's dad touch me inappropriately, my boss hit on me, my boyfriend cheat on me, and now I've sold my Soul to the devil. It was an eventful year for a 16-year-old, wouldn't you say? I want out; living sucks.

I can't even die. I am violently throwing up. I can see the meds in the toilet bowl. Fork, I just want out. I have thrown up so much that I am now sleepy. I hope some meds are still inside me, and I don't wake up tomorrow—no such forking luck. I do sleep in until 3 pm, but I am still alive. What now?

What choice do I have but to go about my shitty life. My next shift isn't for a few days; I've got cash. I'm going to go out and get completely smashed. I am happy and numb, just what I needed. This is the way to take away the pain and escape my reality. I ordered speed for my next shift; it should fly by. My shift is here; guess who comes back and every other shift for weeks. We are getting closer; I am enjoying his visits. The money is really enticing; I am so tempted to switch roles. My boss loves the idea and will offer me a significantly higher split. One of the other girls trains me in erotic massage, and then I see a client with her to witness the end part, what they refer to as a happy ending. The guy is really into it; this looks like a piece of cake. I am making so much money for a girl who is a couple of weeks shy of 17. I am now taking speed every day; I only feel guilty about it when I see my mother. I always bring her a pile of cash; she doesn't ask any questions.

Back at work, I am with Peter, now one of my regular clients. We have spent so much time together, and even though this guy is much older than me, I like him, and I think the feeling is mutual as he asks me out on a lunch date. He takes me to the Sebel Townhouse in Elizabeth Bay, a harbourside inner city suburb in the eastern suburbs of Sydney. The staff greet him by name and know his order. He tells me he comes here often. We laughed, drank wine, had a great time, and enjoyed each other's company. I don't think either of us wanted the date to end. He calls his friend and then asks if I want to go out on a boat this afternoon. I'm trying to act cool, but I'm so excited. I have been on a small fishing boat with my dad, but never on a big one. We drank so much wine at lunch that I needed to straighten up; I went into the bathroom before we left to have a line of speed. There are 3 or 4 guys on the boat. They are all his friends, and they seem lovely. We drink, laugh, listen to music; I am having a great time. One of the guys pulls out Quaaludes. I have never taken this drug before, but everyone else is popping them, so why not? I think I take 2 or 3, and I am having the best time, but now the boat is docking; I have no idea what time it is, but it's dark. Peter invites me back to his place for a drink. We have sex for what seems like hours. We both fall asleep and what feels like a minute later, he is kissing my forehead; it's now morning. He suggests a champagne brunch back at the Sebel Townhouse. No, thank you, I'm in the same clothes. He makes me pancakes instead; they are really good. I can tell he has done this before.

We plan to see each other again that evening, the one after that, and so on. We are now dating, and I stay at his house every night. My things are at his home, and I only go back to my place to pay rent; I don't want to give up my room even though things are going well. This guy spoils me. We go to the Sebel Townhouse regularly; they now know me too, and my regular order of chicken and mashed potato, I'm so fancy, ha! He takes me on his friend's boat several times a week; we attend black-tie events. I am so young and impressionable that it was great for a while until he started getting extremely jealous. He wants me to stop working; I won't do it. The money makes me feel independent. I finally have choices for the first time in my life. I will not be reliant on anyone, especially not a man like my mother has been. Peter isn't happy about my decision, and we are arguing for the first time in our relationship; he even turns up at my work unexpectedly. I broke up with him and took my things back to the sunroom.

The couple I'm living with have been used to their own space, and the girl offers to help me find somewhere else. Quite frankly, they could have told me this before taking my rent money for the last couple of months. Anyhow, it is what it is, and once more, I am looking for another place. The girl finds me a room in a house in Maroubra, which I share with three other young people. They are all guys, but they are super nice. On my first night there, I went down to the Rocks in Sydney with a couple of the guys; we had a pretty big night, and it was a nice welcome. The guys are messy, but other than that, things are going well here. They ask what I do for work; I tell them I work with my grandfather at Trivett Classic BMW; that's where he worked when he retired after 30 years in the police force. They seem to buy it, and we all get along very well.

Peter and I don't speak for a while, but he calls me out of the blue one day. I had already moved on by then, but we stayed close friends for years. We never told anyone where we had met, and we would go out with our different partners together. He also visited my ex-husband's palatial holiday home in Bali, bringing different girls in the adult industry with him each time. We loved the Bali party scene. He even spent Christmas with us there one year, along with my brother and others, and we treated him like part of our family. Towards the end of our friendship, we were so close that we would speak multiple times a day; except for the arguing at the end of our relationship, we always got along very well.

Now I meet another client at work, but during the next few years, I don't have as much recall. I was heavily into drugs by now, so Ill try my best. I know the next two guys went back and forth and even overlapped at times. They knew about each other and kept trying to win me over.

Let's start with the next one, my fun guy; I had never met someone like him with so few inhibitions. If we were in a supermarket and a song came on that he liked, he would dance right there in the aisles. We went clubbing and dancing every weekend; we even made a video clip together at a venue in Darlingharbour; he chose the song Give It Up by KC and The Sunshine Band. I laugh every time I hear that song. He would always take photos of me; no matter where we were, he wasn't embarrassed. We would go for drives and have sex in the car, and if we were in the middle of nowhere and the urge came, we would even have sex outside. We both really enjoyed sex, and one night, he took me to a swingers club. I felt so uncomfortable and wanted to leave, but he coaxed me into having a threesome with another woman. This guy brought me out of my shell so to speak. I thought he was wild and he loved drugs as much as I did. MDMA was our drug of choice.

My fun guy proposed to me, and I said yes. Much to my mother's dismay, she called my other guy I was back and forth with and pleaded with him to get me to break it off. As I wrote this, I thought, why would she have cared? And then it hit me: my other guy would give her money and buy her things; he even purchased her a car.

One day, we were at the Black Market Nightclub in Chippendale, an inner city suburb of Sydney. Day clubs are where you go to continue partying right throughout the day. You go to other clubs at night, getting trashed, head home for a quick freshen-up and back to partying in a seedy day club full of drug fiends and dealers. We rock in high after being out all night, and some of the Bra Boys are there. They are members of a Sydney gang. I know them as they are friends of my other guy.

One of them throws a punch at my fun guy's head; it is so loud I hear it over the music, more and more punches. I am screaming, stop, stop, what the fork are you doing? I scream at the security guards to help. They wander over so slowly; time is standing still, and I can see who is in whose pocket. Never in my life have I witnessed something so terrifying and unprovoked, all because we were in love. I called up my other guy in tears. I could not believe what I had just witnessed; how could you do this? He swears he didn't and promises to talk to the boys to ensure this doesn't happen again. Maybe he didn't know about it, but I bet he didn't shed a tear either. This doesn't break us up, but if I'm honest, in the end, it was the fact that he loved me more than I loved him. It pains me to write that even to this day, he was such a lovely guy and deserved way more than I was giving him. From the bottom of my heart, I'm so sorry. I hope he found a beautiful woman who makes him so happy and fulfilled. She would be one lucky girl. I'm sorry I couldn't be that one.

My other guy was my wise guy and another client I had met at work. We all have relationships that change us and profoundly impact our lives. This was one for me; he will always have a special place in my heart, but it wasn't always like that, so let me start at the beginning. I'm unsure how old or young I was when I first met Les. He came into the massage parlour where I was working. I didn't know who he was, but I knew he was not like all my other clients. He spent a lot of time on the phone and had a massive guy in the waiting room. This guy intrigued me; he returned often, always during the day and didn't wear work attire like my other clients. We talked about everything, our shared love of food; he enjoyed going to restaurants. We chatted about drugs and nightclubs; he told me he wasn't into either. I thought that was because he was older than me, but then he knew of all the clubs I frequented. We discuss everything except what he does for work. Who is this guy?

One day, he told me about one of his favourite restaurants in Surry Hills. I think it was called Taylors, he was raving about it and asked if I would like to go with him. I get asked out a lot at work and, on most occasions, decline, but I was curious and felt I could trust him. He picks me up; this is weird. Another guy is driving. I'm guessing the three of us are going to the restaurant. Nope, the driver waits for us. Once inside, we are ushered to the best table. He orders enough food for the whole restaurant but nothing with red meat; he announces that he doesn't eat it and asks if I would like some. I don't eat much red meat myself, and I think we have more than enough food. Wine? Oh yes, please. What wine would you like? Whatever you're having. He tells me he doesn't drink. This is a first for me. I have never been out with a guy who doesn't drink. He doesn't drink, he doesn't do drugs, and he doesn't go to clubs; what does this guy do for fun? He tells me he likes to gamble. At least he has one vice; I was starting to think I was eating lunch with a goodie two shoes. We had such a nice time and a lovely meal, and he handed me a bag of white powder on the way out. I wonder what he is expecting now. Nothing. Les and his driver dropped me back, and he kissed me on the cheek goodbye. Could a guy I met in a massage parlour really be a gentleman?

I am spending more and more time with Les and enjoying his company. He tells me he had not long gotten out of jail and was on parole, so he was living with a friend in Clovelly, a small beach-side suburb in Sydney's eastern suburbs. I want to know what for; I need to know I haven't been spending time with a rapist or a murderer. He tells me he went to jail for being an SP bookie. I don't know what that is; it doesn't sound that bad. I imagine it has something to do with his love of gambling. We find it hard to spend time alone. He has a flatmate, and I have three. He offers to pay my rent so I can get my own place. He assures me it's my place, and I can do as I please; he will just visit me once or twice a week. I am really considering his generous offer. I like spending time with this guy, and I have never lived alone. I found a two-bedroom apartment in the same suburb I was living in, Maroubra, in the eastern suburbs of Sydney, but this time by the beach. He bought me all the furniture and a budgerigar pet bird I wanted. I am loving this. I can listen to music without disturbing anyone. I can walk around naked. No one is in the shower when I want to use it. I don't have to tidy up after anyone else. I am free to do whatever I want, and so is he. He never visits on the weekends so I can go out all weekend with my friends. Pinch me; this is perfect. I may have been there a year when Les had finished his parole and moved into his own apartment in the same small beach-side suburb he lived in. He had purchased a beautiful apartment in Clovelly with water views as far as the eye could see. I decided to move myself, this time a little closer to him, the suburb next door. I found a lovely apartment in Coogee, another coastal area of the eastern suburbs. Now that I am living closer we spend more and more time together except on the weekends when I go out with my friends. He never invades my privacy by asking where I am or who I am with. I love the freedom, but it does get lonely. I think he could sense my restlessness and discontentment with this so-called relationship and asked me to move in with him.

I moved into his beautiful digs, but the inside looked a little like an older person's home with all the antique furniture. I laugh now when I think of how much he humoured me, and allowed me to change some pieces of his beautiful antique furniture into cheaper modern pieces of crap. In this apartment, life became like nothing I'd ever experienced. Being Les Kalache's girlfriend came with lots of extra benefits. I was just happy to finally feel validated and spend every day with the man I loved, except after hours on weekends, of course. I also don't have to cook or clean, which is perfect as Mum never taught me how. Her speciality was spag bol from a jar. Les knows I can't cook and sometimes prepares a meal for me. My favourite is schnitzel and mashed potato; I'm still so fancy. He was so sure I wouldn't use the oven that I came home one day and told me there was almost a fire. He had hidden something in the oven, forgot, and turned it on. To this day, I don't know what he cooked, but it must have been really important, expensive or both, as he wasn't in the best of moods that night. Some nights, we would get takeaway from restaurants that don't usually offer it, but they would fall over themselves to do it for Les. But as for most nights, we would eat dinner out with his friends; he had so many friends, including people in law enforcement and the legal sector.

Saturday nights were my favourite when he would take a big group for dinner, including my girlfriends. One of our favoured restaurants was an Italian in Darlinghurst; they loved Les and would always fuss over us. We would have a private room, they would play music for us, and we had our own bar to do lines of cocaine on. Well, not him; he didn't do drugs, but he always picked up the tab for everything, including a hefty tip. My girlfriends loved being a part of his entourage. He wasn't into clubs and late nights, so after dinner, I would go out with my friends, and we would pass like ships in the night, but In the wee hours of the morning, I would be getting into bed and Les out. He would get up early. Before going to the gym, he would go to his ex-partner's house to be there when his young son awoke in the morning. He loved him so much, was proud to be his dad, and wanted to give him everything he didn't have as a child. He always spoke about his plans for his son's future and never wanted him to follow in his footsteps. Hand on heart, I never knew precisely what his footsteps were. I wasn't stupid; I knew it was shady because he had plenty of money and drugs but never went to work. Les had a big antique desk he would sit at most of the day, and people would come to him. If I ever came home from work and someone was still there, they would take the conversation outside. I was never privy to anything. Every time, I would question something. I was told to drop it; it was for my own good. I honestly thought it was because he didn't trust me. He also took cold showers every day to prepare for the possibility of being sent back to jail. This scared me no end, the thought of losing the man I love. I would plead with him, let's go and leave this life behind. His response was, I have too many mouths to feed; people depend on me. That's Les always thinking about others; I wonder if, in hindsight, if he wished he would have listened to me. What am I saying? There is no way that man would have ever held me back from reaching my destiny.

Back to Saturday nights, occasionally, between the group and I, we could talk him into joining us at a club before he would head home for his slumber. This is when you felt like a celebrity. The owners would come out to greet us, offer us drinks, and couldn't do enough for us. I remember at the Cauldron Nightclub in Darlinghurst, one night, a bunch of us doing lines right off the bar in plain sight of all the staff and patrons. No one said a peep; no one ever said a word to Les Kalache. He had gotten me memberships to all the clubs I loved to go to, but him coming out with me was the royal treatment on another level.

I also ceased the massage job and was told I did not have to work at all. I love my independence, and even though money was not an object for the first time in my life, I wanted to work and decided to get a real job. I still don't have the experience, but somehow, I managed to land a job as a personal assistant for a woman in the tanning industry. Tina has a few salons and an import business; she takes me under her wing and teaches me the ropes. I'm in awe; she is one savvy businesswoman. I love this job. I have been here a while and on top of my P.A duties, I also run one of the tanning centres. One day, I think this is an easy business; the money the centre makes, the staff is the highest cost, and there is very little inventory, only a few sachets of tanning cream. I will open one, and if I do most of the work, there go the staff costs. I discussed this with Les; he thinks it's a great idea, believes in me, and will lend me the money.

Now I need to talk to my boss, who imports the best tanning beds. Tina isn't happy that she is losing me but is impressed with my drive; I remind her of herself at a younger age. We are all set then. I have 50%, Les 40%, and I give 10% of the company to my friend Cheryl. In return she will help me with the business and work some of the long hours. We open up, and Cheryl and I have the time of our lives until we face financial problems. I didn't factor in paying back the costly tanning beds. Tina's business owned their beds, and I never wrote cheques for the monthly money we pay. Two previously happy-go-lucky girls were now two stressed out, no fun at all girls. I know it was my fault that Cheryl left; I wasn't a nice person to be around anymore. I have now lost not only a working business partner but my partner in crime.

I am now more stressed than ever. Les becomes distant, and we are arguing all the time. I am trying so hard; I want this business to work. I know the money doesn't matter to

Les, but it's the fact he believed in me; I want to make him proud. A friend I haven't seen in ages calls me out of the blue. She asks me if I'm sitting down; yes, why? What's going on? Is everything alright? Are you ok? She tells me she has seen Les with another girl; they were in a big group but were really close. I don't jump to conclusions; I know my man and think there must be an explanation. I call him straight up. Les, you said we would never lie to each other, so tell me the truth. Were you with another girl in Coogee? Yes, yes, I was, and I'm sorry. I can't believe what I hear; my whole world just crashed. Who is she? How long has it been going on? You were in a big group, so others know too. He tells me that he met her at one of his early morning training sessions. He is so sorry; it has been happening for a while, and he didn't know how to tell me.

I'm having an outer body experience. I can see myself; my heart is beating through my chest, I can't breathe, and I can't think straight. I put a sign on the door. Emergency had to close early today, and I got in my car and drove to his apartment, which we shared. He is outside in the street; something inside me just snapped. I have no idea what I'm doing. The next minute, I'm reaching into my car for my club lock, and I start beating him with it. He covers his head and takes my beating. Looking back, he could have stopped me instantly but let me get out my seething rage. I am not proud of many moments in my life, but that one takes the cake. I then walk upstairs and start packing everything into my car. He keeps telling me, please don't go; you don't have to leave. Like fork, I don't. I hadn't for a minute considered

I had nowhere to go; at this point, adrenaline was the only thing keeping me going.

I return to my tanning salon and put my things in an empty room. There isn't a bed or a shower, but I do have a toilet; I'll have to find somewhere quick smart. I can't believe I'm back here again with nowhere to live. My mind is racing, thinking about how I did not see the signs. I have been so stressed trying to build this business up and make him proud, and all the while, he has been getting it on with some other chick. I have been cheated on before, but this one cut way deeper. If I look closely, I think it was the fact that I had never felt so protected; my parents hadn't protected me, and I knew with all my heart he would never let anyone hurt me. Not in my wildest dreams did I think he would be the one inflicting the pain. I think a part of me died that day; I now forking hate him so much.

Les not being a drinker or partier meant that I only really did it with friends on the weekends, but now I'm angry and alone. I find somewhere to live, and I go out all the time. I have nothing to do with that man unless I speak with him about business. He is worried about me, burning the candle at both ends and has asked my mum to help me with the business. I don't know what he said because she wouldn't have done it if I had requested it. He also told me he had won an apartment in a card game near my business and would like me to live there to make my life a little easier. I think, ok, fork it; that's the least you can do. I also wonder how someone could gamble away an apartment; some people are truly mad. I moved into the two-bedroom apartment, painted the walls a dusky pink colour, had a white couch, it's all very girly, and he also organised a cleaner to help me out. I can see he is trying. We talk more now, but I also know he is still seeing the affair girl. I then come up with a horrendous plan. Les and I start sleeping together again, soon after, he announces that he has gotten rid of the other girl and wants to be together again. I am so happy my plan has worked; he is alone. I look him dead in the eye and say, "Fork you, as if, does it feel good, hey?" That was so cruel of me, but I felt satisfied knowing that he also was humiliated. To this day, I will never forget the smirk on his face; Les knew he had been played. I believe this was the moment when I earned Les Kalche's respect. Our love had now changed into a deep, unconditional bond that has lasted for years.

My next relationship was with my good-in-bed guy. I met him in a nightclub in Kings Cross. We had an intense sexual chemistry that I had never experienced before. He turned me on like no one else and had a massive sex drive. I could never say no to him; he had power over me, and I was weak in his presence. We cannot keep our hands off each other; we have sex all the time. Just like me, he liked clubs and dancing too. We would go out every weekend. Dancing and sex was the only thing on the menu. I don't know if we had anything else in common, but who cared? We didn't have any free time. I moved out of my girly apartment and into his apartment in Randwick. My boyfriend takes steroids and has a buff bod. I wonder if it works on women, I want to try too. He stabs me in the butt every day with the anabolic steroid Stanozolol. It doesn't work for me like it does for him; he is a gym junkie, and I hate the gym.

I just get bigger and angrier. My wise guy Les finds out and isn't happy. He trains every day for fitness; it's a mental thing for him. The body is just a by-product. So now he doesn't like my boyfriend for giving it to me, but I didn't care. It was none of his business.

Speaking of business, my old boss Tina had offered to buy my tanning business. Finally, I can be free; this was way tougher than I had envisioned. Les gets paid back, and I think about what's next. Maybe a beauty salon, so I decided to study beauty therapy. I found a private college in Paddington, but the tuition is very expensive. I asked Les for the money, and he obliged. I go around one afternoon to collect the big bag of cash. Whilst I'm there, my boyfriend calls. I'm just at Les' place; I'll be back soon. I return home, and he is so angry. He asks why I was there and accuses me of wanting him back. I am not about to explain myself. Does he not understand that we would be back together if we had wanted to be? With God as my witness, it wasn't like that anymore. Looking back, I now see that it would be hard to understand the bond Les and I share. That's another reason I love and appreciate Les' current girlfriend, apart from the fact she is a beautiful Soul and genuinely loves him. She has never questioned our love for each other; that girl has her head on her shoulders. It warms my heart that he has found someone who loves and makes him so happy. I have a beautiful praying Angel ornament that the couple gave me. In all the years that I have known Les, it is, without a doubt, the most beautiful gift I have ever received. I cherish it; it sits in my meditation area and always makes me smile.

Back in Randwick at my boyfriend's. I will not put up with being spoken to in this manner. I grab an overnight bag and leave for the Crowne Plaza in Coogee. In the morning, I will start looking at apartments for rent that are available immediately. We break up, but this is not the end of us for good; in the next few years, we gravitate towards each other again and again. I said this guy had power over me, and I could not resist his charms, but I'm angry at him for now, and I took an apartment in Coogee. The rent for my apartment is killing me. I'm only a student now. I discussed with Les that I need weekend work that pays well. He offered to pay my rent to help me out, regardless of what happened between us. He loves me and doesn't want to see me do it tough again. I know he can afford it, so I say thank you. I really appreciate his kindness; some ex-partners want to see you struggle and fail when you are no longer together.

I was single for a while before I met my next guy through a buddy I had dated long ago. It's honestly hard to remember exactly when my buddy and I dated. It was brief, and we were really good friends for so many years, at times in our younger years, going out together every weekend. Two things I remember about our short-lived relationship are that we took a trip together—not a pack-your-suitcases kind of trip, but an LSD acid trip. I also remember the house I lived in. I can work it out. Our relationship was between Peter and my fun guy many moons ago. I remember the trip so vividly because I hated it: to this day, I have never taken another.

I thought others were trying to answer my home phone; yes, we had home phones in those days, ha! Why I thought this and why I cared, your guess is as good as mine, but I ripped the phone socket out of the wall to be safe. Next was shower time because we were going out. This was the worst shower of my life; the water coming out was spiders. My buddy guy had to tell me it was just water and thought we shouldn't go. I was determined I was going; no one could stop me. We arrive at a seedy nightclub in Kings Cross. People scare me when walking by me; they look and move as fast as the cartoon Road Runner. I jump out of their way so they don't run me over; that must have been a sight. My next stop before home is McDonald's; I am starving. I order so much food, and when consuming it, I can feel it moving throughout my body. Now, for the best part of the night. We arrived back at the Maroubra house that I shared with three other flatmates, and I sat outside in the front yard, flopped up against the house. Here, I cry my heart out for hours, upon hours, upon hours; this trip is never-ending. I can only imagine what the neighbours thought, let alone my flatmates. For months after, at the most inappropriate times, I would get LSD flashbacks. I never felt like repeating this night; it was pure hell.

The next thing I remember about our relationship is how we broke up. Remember the Black Market Nightclub that hosts a day club on the weekend? Well, on Thursday nights, it was Hellfire, a BDSM Fetish night. An erotic night of Bondage/Discipline, Dominance/Submission, Sadism/Masochism and more. I never got involved, and you know that's the truth, as I have been blatantly honest about so many things. I would go there to party. He was a milkman who had to work very early on Friday morning's and didn't want me to go without him. He called me up with an ultimatum. You go to Hellfire night, and we are over. I can't believe this guy; how dare he. I'll make it easy for you. Fork off. We remained friends for years after; I even attended his wedding. He met his wife when he had left behind his milkman days and joined the corporate world. I love the couple, but the higher up the corporate ladder he went, the less humble they both became. I loved humble milkman, except for the ultimatums!

It's now late 1997, and Les' birthday rolls around; he is five days after mine. I called him to wish him a happy birthday, but there was no answer. When he still hadn't called me back the next day, I thought he must have had a problem with his phone. I took his birthday present to his apartment, but there was no answer. This is unlike Les; I drive to his friend's apartment in Coogee, and they haven't seen him. I called some of his friends, but no one had seen him. I'm worried now; I imagine the worst.

The following day, I got a call from one of his friends; his solicitor had called. Les is in jail; the police picked him up on his birthday. He has been remanded to Silverwater prison, where they take people who haven't been convicted yet. No one has been able to speak with him. I feel sick, and I can't breathe, but at the same time, I'm relieved that he is alive. This was not a random act; friends of his, including law enforcement officers, were also getting raided left, right and centre and taken to jail. I now understand that a special task force was set up and given the name Operation Gymea, one of the largest operations ever conducted against organised criminals.

People were coming to me and telling me he was a dog and giving people up. I get into a screaming match with one woman. I know Les, there is no way he would tell the cops anything; get out of my face. I don't understand why all these people keep saying this. There is no way in hell he would do that. I wish he would call me; I wish he would call someone, anyone. A few days later, he finally called. They had him locked up in solitary confinement whilst they carried out the raids on his friends. He is worried about my rent money. The Crimes Commission has frozen all his assets. He will get a friend to sort it out. I tell him are you mad? Don't worry about me; I'll work it out. I'm fine; I'm out here. I'm worried about you. I can't believe what people say; I know you would never. What's going on? The police had recordings they had played him before they stuck him in solitary so he couldn't warn anyone. Les spent his birthday night in jail alone. It was later revealed that quite a while before, when he had Foxtel installed, listening devices were planted in the roof of his penthouse apartment. There was also a Royal Commission investigation into the crimes, and the raids didn't stop there; they continued in waves. I think I was in the last wave long after Les' arrest, but for now, let's stay in 1997.

I have never felt grief like this; you are grieving the loss of someone who is still alive. The thought of him stuck inside that place is killing me. I am so stressed; I can hear him speak to me; hey, kiddo, and I turn around expecting him to be there, but he's not; he is in that awful place, and who knows for how long. I worry about other inmates and if he is hungry or cold. I know he is tough and will be okay, but no one wants to see someone they love lose their freedom. The stress is too much; I have severe acne all over my forehead. I had broken out in the same spot years ago while going through puberty, and a six-month course of the now-banned Accutane did the job. It doesn't work this time. Luckily, I wear a fringe, I try everything, but nothing works, then finally I find a Chinese herbalist and start to see some improvement. YAY, I'm going to stick to these stinky herbal drinks. While all this is happening, I also need to find weekend work. I want to pay my own rent. I know Les would sort it out for me, but I don't want to add any extra burden to his life right now.

I land a weekend job as a door bitch at Q Bar, a nightclub in Oxford St, Sydney. My buddy guy introduced me to his friend, that works in security there and helped me to get the job. This guy is kind and teaches me the ropes, including tips to be more authoritative. He introduces me to all the staff so they can look after me. I also get a walkie-talkie connected to all the security guys in case of trouble. This is a great job; it pays well, it's fun, all the owners, bosses and staff are cool, and taking drugs at work is not frowned upon. It's not officially allowed, but everyone knows everyone else is doing it. After we close, usually during daylight hours, we have staff drinks. This is the best job ever; you get paid for being in a club. My new work friend and I started hanging out more and more; we are becoming very good mates. I usually go to the beach after work, swim and fall asleep on the sand, but not today; after staff drinks, my mate announces he would like to keep partying. He has a huge bag of cocaine. He asks, where can we go?

We head to my apartment in Coogee. We do line after line after line. We are so high, and this guy smokes cigarettes; I don't have a balcony, so my lounge room stinks. I gave up years ago but fork it, I'm going to have one too. I'm so embarrassed about the acne on my forehead, but I have to take off this disgusting makeup that has been on all night. I come out of the bathroom all shy, and he tells me I look beautiful. I thought that was so sweet. I don't think about the fact he was high as a kite. Then he kissed me, and I liked it. We continued kissing and doing lines all day until the early evening when he had to go back to work with his blue balls, ha!

We are now spending all our free time together. We keep it quiet at work and try to act professionally, but some staff can see how protective he is over me. His beautiful brother works on the door, too; we get along so well that we always go out with him and his girlfriend. I also got to meet his other brother. I absolutely love these guys. They are Samoan New Zealanders and as tough as nails to others, but they are big teddy bears to me. They are so protective and treat me like their little sister. I have fallen in love with his family, too. It's now time to meet his parents; I'm excited as his brothers are such beautiful Souls, and I imagine they are as well. His mother is such a sweet woman; I love her. I don't have much to say about his dad, so let's just say I can see who the boys take after. We spent so much time with each other that we decided to move in together. We found an apartment in Poplar St in Darlinghurst, only metres away from Oxford St and the club where we work. It is so close we have people back to ours after work all the time.

Fast forward many months down the track. We were lying in bed one morning when the home phone rang; it was the police who told me to open the door immediately. I opened it, embarrassed that wine bottles were everywhere from the night before. There are two detectives and a group of officers. I ask, what's going on? Is Les ok? They have a search warrant for the premises. They just woke me up; I need to pee, and a woman officer follows me into the bathroom to watch me. This is insanity. They are searching the place, going through absolutely everything. I am shitting myself; I have a stash of speed hidden in the heels of my shoes. They are going through my cupboard, pulling everything out; the shoes are coming out. I think I'm going to have a heart attack, but I have to act cool, FORK!!!!!!!!!!!! I'm a drug user, not a dealer; with Les inside, this strong stuff is hard to come by. I wouldn't share any of it, but I bet they wouldn't believe me.

Phew, I have never been more relieved; they stop searching; they are satisfied there is nothing here, but I still need to come down to the station. I didn't understand why and asked my boyfriend to call Les' Barrister. I am taken to Surry Hills Police Station, and not long after, the QC Barrister arrives. I don't understand what's happening. Ken Madden, the Barrister, is one of the kindest men I have ever met. He was so caring and supportive during one of my lowest times. He explains that I am being held on a conspiracy drug charge, and I will need to appear in court so a trial date can be set. He gets me out on bail, so I don't have to be in jail until then. I'm absolutely numb; how can this be happening? Les never told me anything, and now I understand what he meant when he would say it was for my own good. He was protecting me, after all.

The following years are so stressful, not knowing if you will be going to jail. I constantly have nightmares about it. All I do is eat, and I drink two bottles of cheap wine a night. I have become an alcoholic and blown up like a balloon. I pretend all is okay. I don't want to worry anyone, and I don't want my grandfather to find out. I have become a shell of the woman I once was. It's also hard to hold a job when you must take time off to attend court. I was so blessed that I was close to Tina, my old boss, and I could be honest with her about my situation and why I needed time off. She sympathised with me and offered me a job at the head office. Tina and my boyfriend were the only ones I could talk to. I had numerous court appearances leading up to my trial date because my Barrister hoped that the other cases charged under the same task force would be heard first. This way, I wouldn't be grouped together with all the naughty people.

I'm glad someone believes I'm innocent. Over time, all the cases are getting heard, and so many jail sentences are dished out, including Les' 22-year sentence. Now, everyone finally knows what I know: he isn't a dog. I'm in complete shock and disbelief people don't get that long for murder. I am absolutely terrified for my trial. I'm not built for jail. I can't recall exactly how long my trial date was set after being charged, but it's here and felt like a lifetime. On day one, the jury is chosen. On days two, three, and most of day four, I kept getting asked the same questions repeatedly, in different ways. They are asking me to remember things I said ages ago and what I meant by them. I kept getting handed sheets of paper with transcripts of what they thought I had said and then playing the recordings, which were found to be wrong. One I had supposedly spoken about, they were suggesting I had all this weed. I didn't know what they were talking about; weed has never been my drug of choice.

My Barrister asked them to play the recording, and I laughed when I heard myself, which was inappropriate in court. I was speaking about a dream I had had the night before. In my bogan accent, I clearly said the word dream; they should have had a bogan translator. What a riveting conversation, ask anyone who knows me; I could talk underwater. It's almost the end of day four; the case is put to rest, we have had closing arguments, and the jury has gone to deliberate. My Barrister warns me that, more than likely, the case will go over till the next day but to stay close. I can honestly say I have never been more petrified in my entire life.

Waiting, I don't speak to anyone. I have no words. I feel like I'm going to faint. I go to the bathroom to throw up and wipe off all the sweat. I look in the mirror, and I'm white as a ghost. I have to give myself a pep talk; I have to be strong. I may be going straight to a women's prison from here. We are all shocked, the jury has reached a verdict earlier than expected. My Barrister advises that I am to keep it together no matter what the result. My heart is pounding; my legs aren't working as I try to approach the court table. I have no idea how the inmates on death row can walk to their execution. It feels like time has stood still as I watch the jury hand the bailiff the paper for the Judge. It's like watching the TV show Law and Order: Has the jury reached a verdict, etc.? However, my freedom is at stake in this episode. After what felt like the longest time in history, I finally heard the words not guilty.

In my mind, I have a second chance at life; my boyfriend proposes to me, and I say yes. I love him and his brothers; we have become a very close-knit family, and he has shown me how supportive he can be. I think he will make a great husband. Now that I am not on bail, I'm free to do so much more. We booked a trip to Bali; I was so excited. I had never been overseas, though we never got to go, in the end, we couldn't afford it. We also plan to open a business together; I can visit Les in jail. My fiancé is very supportive and drives me the long way to see Les in the Australian super-maximum prison In Goulburn. You have to cut through a lot of red tape and go through security measures before being allowed inside. The prison officers are not the friendliest bunch and seem unhurried about getting you to your pre-booked visit, especially after your long drive from Sydney. To their credit, it must be a tough job. Finally, you are allocated a table number and told to sit there and wait. I look around at all the other inmates and visitors; some of the visitors seem like wives and girlfriends. I can tell by the conversations I can hear. I think about Les cheating on me; if he hadn't, I know myself and the love I have for him. I too, would have endured a 22-year sentence.

Now, it's for the affair chick to endure, but she doesn't. I forgot to mention they got back together and married whilst he was in prison, but she cheated on him, and they got a divorce. Even though I understand it was his Karma to bear, I feel bad for him. It's sad to hear that, especially when he is at his lowest. I wonder if she has been dished her Karma yet; we can never avoid it.

Back in the prison visitors room, I see parents and children; how sad it must be to visit a parent in jail. How would kids understand why their father is in jail? I also see other prisoners behind glass panels but don't stare. I wonder what they are in for. Les is here for 22 years and is allowed a table. Finally, a prison officer brings him through a door, and he comes to greet me. It is heartbreaking to see him like this; he has shaved his head and looks thinner. I have to hold back my tears. Les can tell I'm sad, and he assures me he is okay. He is chatting to me and other inmates like we are in a bloody café full of his friends. Is he just putting on a brave face for me, or has he made this his home? The visit flies by, and the next minute, I'm hugging Les goodbye; this is when I can no longer hold back my tears; they are streaming down my face. How can I walk back outside into the real world, leaving him behind? This is torture. Thank goodness, I have my fiancé waiting for me in the car. I also let him know that next time he is coming in with me, Les would like to meet him.

We continue with our plans to open a business together. We decided on a security business since my fiancé already has contacts in the industry. He has a criminal record, so he can't hold a master licence, which is required to operate. I applied, and it was granted. Here we go. Our first security contract was with Q Bar, where we once both worked. It is hard for me now as I need to adhere to the legal requirements, and when an incident is reported to the police, I am expected to have all the information in the reports. This is our livelihood; if I lose my master licence, what then? He can't seem to understand my feelings of responsibility and continues to take the side of his security boys, which causes friction between us. We get lots more contracts, start installing alarms and get a government contract to train students.

The business is growing, and we have moved into a beautiful office on Wentworth Avenue in Sydney. The best part of being in that office is that it's a family affair; his brothers work for us, and mine too. I do all the books and payroll, and my fiancé looks after the contracts. We have a cash flow problem; we don't get paid before we have to pay our large payroll every Friday. It was very stressful; I would be harassing late payers and going without wages myself anything just to make it happen. I always found a way to pull the rabbit out of the hat. He didn't have to deal with this and didn't understand how tough it was. He would spend much-needed funds. We never argued at work, but one day, I had enough. I had done everything to ensure the funds were in the account for the Friday wages. I went to the bank to collect the cash; I was informed there were insufficient funds. What do you mean it was there not long ago when I checked? There was a withdrawal; there were only two signatories, and it wasn't me. I find him in the filing room. I ask WTF. He said he needed something; I explained that he should have asked first as the funds were there to cover the wages, and I don't know where I will find the money now. He responded that it's your department and your problem to fix. It doesn't stop there; we lose contracts and downsize.

There are only contractors and him, and I are in another smaller office.

Things are still tight, and I take on a full-time job in real estate; I figure I can go to the office after hours to keep up my duties. He doesn't like answering the phone now and hires his baby brother to do it. I love his bro, but are you serious? I am now working full-time, going to the office after hours to complete my duties, including payroll, which I now have one more to add to the list. Typing this today, I can't believe I didn't tell him to go fork himself right then; healed Michelle would have. Unhealed, Michelle continues to love him, tries to see his point of view and makes excuses for his bad behaviour. This went on for years, and at one point, I joined in on the who gives a toss about responsibilities behaviour and put a boob job on my credit card. I have the same saline implants today. They are supposed to be changed every ten years, but I have never been able to afford it.

I've had it; I can't take it anymore. I want out of the business. He can keep it. I am going to TAFE to study financial services full-time. He needs to find someone to take over the master licence; from memory, I think he got his middle brother to do it. I'm so happy; I feel free, and I no longer have to fight with my fiancé over the business. We see things so differently. The business covers our rent and bills. I receive student payments from the government, which pays for groceries and fresh food. In this relationship, I cook. I'm not great, to say the least, but my fiancé doesn't complain, and neither does my brother, who comes over for dinner every night.

Seb moved from Tasmania a little while back to an apartment I had found and furnished for him with my fiancé's help; I love how family-orientated he is. Seb's pad was only a street over from ours. I now get to concentrate on looking after our home and my studies, which I'm enjoying. I have even received a few distinctions I'm so proud of; I worked very hard for them. Studying doesn't come easily for me; I am not book-smart like some students. My feeling free didn't last long; I only got to study for two terms when, one afternoon after college, I went to put my key in the door of our apartment in Newtown, but it didn't work. I then found a notice from the sheriff's office that we had been evicted. I have no idea how long he hadn't paid the rent for. We had to stay in a hotel that night and find another home. I swore I would never be back here, not having a place to live. I forgave him, and we stayed together after that; but after everything, if I'm honest, this was the beginning of the end. Being kicked out of my home had shaken me to the core.

Now, I start to spiral out of control. I became a very angry, I couldn't see a way out; I'm in love with an irresponsible person. I started drinking even more and would have got a DUI if I hadn't seen the booze bus ahead, pulled the car over and ran into a hedge to hide. The cops found me and asked me to take a breath analysis, which I declined; I was charged with refusing to submit a breath analysis. I had become a horrible person and an absolute smart arse. I'm sorry, Grandpa, but it gets worse. I'm so ashamed to say that I also got into a fight with a guy who was a security guard, and I was charged with assault. I was at a pub in George St, Sydney, with my fiancé and a couple of others when I popped outside for a cigarette; I went to go back inside and was denied. I argued with the bouncer that my man, handbag and phone were inside. He didn't give a shit, and the next minute, I was swinging punches, and the police were called. My ego justified my despicable behaviour by saying he should have let me back in to gather my things, or he should have got them for me; you can't leave a girl out on the street with no belongings, etc. I came up with plenty of excuses. I'm so sorry, Three Wise Monkeys security guard; there are no excuses for physical violence. You were right to deny me access; I was drunk.

I was blessed that once again, Les' Barrister supported me, explained the recent stress in my life, and obtained a section 10. This meant I was still found guilty of the offence, but no conviction was recorded, so I don't have a criminal record. I now get a job at a bank and work full-time as a teller at Westpac. I enjoyed this job, but it doesn't pay enough to put aside savings and pay all my bills. I need to save as I am planning my exit strategy. I think my fiancé is sensing me pulling away as he is getting angry and aggressive. I had never judged him on his dad's behaviour (his dad used to beat him, his mum and his beautiful brothers), but now I am starting to think twice. His behaviour is escalating; I need to move quickly. I call my friend Peter; he knows people in the adult industry. Do you know of any reception jobs going? He introduced me to Misty; she has an erotic massage parlour in Bondi Junction, next door to a friend, Lilith's parlour, whom I met through Peter.

It's perfect. Misty works nights, and there is a casual employee along with another day receptionist with whom I have become close. She only works a few shifts, so I have four-day shifts a week. I can earn much better money and save quickly. I always manage to hit my commission targets, and I save well. I haven't been here long and already have my bond money for an apartment. I need a two bedroom as my brother is moving back from interstate. Bond check: now I need to save a little more for furniture. The other day receptionist and I got on well and decided to get the casual to cover one of our shifts so we could go to lunch together. We get on like a house on fire, and lunch turns into partying all night and the sun coming up. I return home to the townhouse I share with my fiancé in Roseberry, and he is livid. I have never seen him this angry; he grabs me by the throat and pins me up against the wall; my feet are dangling mid-air. I think he is going to choke me to death. I calmed him down and ran upstairs, throwing my clothes into garbage bags, and bolted out the door. Financially, I wasn't ready to go, but it felt like it was now or never.

I very quickly found an apartment in Bondi. The rent was reasonable, and I honestly didn't give two shits what it looked like. It was available, so I took a lease. In most breakups, you have a period of grief, but no, I'm sorry, I still loved him but was more relieved I was safe. I have no idea how I remained friends with him after this; the only word that comes to mind is stupid. I was there for him when his father passed and also when his beautiful baby brother passed. Rest in Peace. I also let him borrow my car while I was on my first overseas trip with my ex-husband, which he crashed and wrote off. I only had 3rd party insurance, and he didn't pay me one cent to help me get a replacement vehicle.

I wasn't special; he also had an accident in my buddy guy's car. His wife wasn't impressed when he also didn't pay them for the damages. Typing all this makes me realise that stupid definitely fits the bill.

We did have some good times together, but the bad ones outweighed them, so I immediately started going out and having fun. I made friends with some working girls on my day shifts, and we would go out for drinks after work; my friend Lilith from next door would come along, too. She was the only one with a partner, Andrew, the same one she has today, but he travelled a lot with work. It was girls' night, almost every night, and I dated a few guys before settling down with my ex-husband. There was the great cook guy, the famous cricketer, the New York banker, and one I was particularly fond of, the coke addict/dealer.

My boss, Misty, and my friend, Lilith, were competitors and had no love for each other. I knew this and would never discuss Misty's business with Lilith, though I never understood why they felt this way. They both had different clientele. Lilith had most of the older, wealthier clients and a smaller percentage of the younger, fun-party clients. Misty had more of the younger, fun-party clients and a smaller percentage of the older, wealthier ones. I never saw the point of the fighting and the ongoing battle between the two women. At Misty's, many regular clients would sometimes pop into the office for a quick chat. One guy would come by quite often and always had his guitar with him; I wonder if he would serenade the ladies; anyhow, I thought he was very cool.

One day, we were chatting, and he said he was having a party that evening and would like me to come. I declined, and then he said he would pay the outcall rates directly and assured me I would only be hanging out with him and his friends, and no one would be aware that I was working. Maybe if my boss said yes, you would have to speak to her. I wouldn't go directly and cut her out. Misty gives the okay, and then I'm nervous. I like the guy, but it's not a date; I'm getting paid. I get home and go through my cupboard. How does one dress for this? I reminded myself it was not a date, so I chose a sundress and flat shoes. I arrived at the party in Dover Heights, in the eastern suburbs of Sydney, looked around at the other guests and was relieved I had dressed casually. He introduced me to his friends. I thought they were all cool, and then he took me inside. In the front room, everyone sits around a big plate full of white powder; he offers me some coke. Thank you. Hell yes, we do a few lines, and then he takes me to another room and plays his guitar for me: he does serenade his ladies.

He pulls out another plate, and we continue to do lines of cocaine, sitting in this same spot for hours, chatting about anything and everything. We like the same music, and he also loves the Red Hot Chilli Peppers. I am having a blast, but it's late. I have to go; I'm working tomorrow. I had so much fun; I can't believe I was given so many drugs and got paid, plus given a hefty tip. I would have come here for free if I had known how much fun it would be.

A few nights later, he called my boss. He would like to book me for an outcall again, but this time for a massage. I was at home having a wine when Misty called me. I think she was expecting me to say no; she seemed surprised when I agreed. Like most others, Misty had no idea I had worked in the industry before; this was my heavily guarded secret. I thought, why not? He was hot and cool and loved drugs. What better way to spend my Saturday night taking drugs with a guy I liked? He would book me repeatedly, and that's when Misty came up with an idea. She had many clients like him, and I wouldn't have to work in the rooms or from the office; she would call me with bookings. This offer was enticing; outcalls pay more than in the rooms, and this time, I'm older and wiser. I could make enough money to purchase everything I need for my apartment and save for a business. I would finally be out of this industry for good. That's when, once again, I swapped sides of the desk, became Michaela and was dubbed the outcall queen.

This job was easy; most of the party clients you would sit around getting high with; they loved how fun Michaela was to hang out with and would keep calling to extend the booking. In these environments your clothes would be on for most of the time. Occasionally, I'd even take cocaine with me; I could get this seriously strong stuff from a dealer I was hanging out with at the time. It was so strong that they would get even higher and keep you there longer and longer. I thought that it was such easy money. I'd do drugs with my friends anyway, but they paid for the drugs and my time. I thought I had it all figured out. I had regulars that I would hang out with, so you get to know them quite well, and you think of them as your mates. It shows how much your ego wants to justify your behaviour. I was lying to myself that I was sitting around with my buddies, taking drugs and getting paid. Everything was going well for a while. I would work four shifts in a row. On those days, I would get high with most clients, finish work in the wee hours, sleep all day and wake in the late afternoon. Eat a big bowl of pasta, my only meal for the day. Drink wine, do lines, and start all over again. I liked it this way: it gave me three nights off for massive party nights with my friends.

As far as everyone knew, I was still a receptionist. I had many regular clients, and one of my favourites lived in the exclusive Gladswood Gardens cul-de-sac in Double Bay; his apartment was a stone's throw from the harbour. One night, we were partying with his flatmate. My client kept extending and extending and extending. I felt terrible; he was such a nice guy. I genuinely liked him, and I hadn't even brushed up against him, let alone taken my clothes off or massaged him. I decided to knock off, stay there, and party with them for free. His flatmate wanted a girl to party with, too. I knew his flatmate well; I had spent much time there, and Misty had a couple of new girls I thought he would like. I rattled off the names for him to ask for when he called. Misty knew I was still there; I didn't think about how he would have known about the new girls; I just wanted to help.

Hand on heart, I was not charging my favourite client and cutting her out. I may be many things, but I'm not a thief and never have been. Misty was pissed and suspended me for two weeks. During these two weeks off, my biopsy result came back from the gynaecologist. I had Cin 3, cervical intraepithelial neoplasia grade 3. A sexually transmitted infection usually causes it. I now understand that it means that there are severely abnormal cells on the surface of the cervix, and if left untreated, it may become cancer and spread to nearby normal tissue. All I heard was cancer, and I thought I was going to die. I kept thinking, If only I had regular pap smears, I could have detected it earlier.

Since I thought I was going to die anyway, my partying escalated even more than usual. I am spending more time hanging out with my coke addict/dealer, and he knows how to party, that's for sure. He would make his lines so big most people would take that amount over the whole night, not to mention how strong his stuff was. You would go from zero to a thousand on one line. He was so addicted; at the end of the night, he would have his last line and fall asleep five minutes later, whilst I was wired as fork. He was always very generous; he wouldn't just take care of my drugs while I was with him. He would give me plenty to take home and pop by with some if needed. My brother loved him coming over, as he would look after him too. He always had the best coke; was cute, and we got along very well.

I could talk to many people, but it felt like he really listened. He was such a sweetheart and always knew what to say. One night, he was being particularly sweet, and I looked at him and said, "You know what? I'm fond of you." He laughed, then looked me in the eyes and said "I'm fond of you too." From then on, that became our thing. He would phone me and say "I'm fond of you," and I'd reply, "I'm fond of you too."

One day, because I was off work, I went with him to a hotel so he could prepare a drop-off. He had booked a hotel in the city under a fake name and pulled out all the drugs to get ready. I have never seen so much in my life. He was getting all the white powder ready and was receiving phone calls; he was running late. He had got the package ready but hadn't cleaned up. I said go, it's ok, I'll do it. He said, thank you, and please don't take it. Sure, and he leaves. All this cocaine is sitting in front of me; how could I clean it up and not have a line? He has the strongest, so I will make a tiny line. As soon as I take it, something is wrong. My heart is beating through my chest, I can hardly breathe, I'm cold and clammy, and I feel like I'm going to pass out. I bolt out to a taxi; I feel like I am going to die. Something is seriously wrong. I am screaming at the taxi driver. Please get me to the nearest hospital, please please. I feel like I'm going to die. He was lovely and got me to the emergency at Sydney Hospital in Macquarie St, only streets away from the hotel. I never thanked him; from the bottom of my heart, thank you, Mr taxi driver; you helped save my life.

In the emergency department, they immediately took my vitals, asked questions, and gave me medication through a catheter. I am told this will go directly into my bloodstream, and I should start feeling better soon. They still needed to monitor my health, and I was given a hospital bed. I had been upfront about taking the line of cocaine, but they still wanted to run tests. Later that evening, when my brother arrived, the results were back. I had a heroin overdose. I wasn't aware my guy dealt heroin, too; he never told me. He knew I was a coke addict; what was he thinking, leaving all that white powder in front of me? Seriously? I had never taken heroin before, but now I can add that to the long list of drugs I have taken.

My two-week suspension is up, and I'm back at work. My nights were usually full, but not now. Misty was obviously sending other girls to the clients because she was always so busy. You would have thought she would appreciate all the extended bookings. Misty showed me who the boss was. I had no idea how long she would hold this grudge, and I needed money. I spoke to my friend Lilith, who owned the erotic massage parlour next door to Misty's in Bondi Junction. I was always hesitant to work for Lilith because her girls were notorious for doing extras, and Misty would fire her girls if she found out. I loved Misty's no-extras policy.

Of course, you had the odd client who would ask, but Misty was tough and trained her clients well. I have seen her throw guys out of the rooms herself for harassing girls; she was one tough bitch. Lilith understood my stance on extras and informed her staff not to send those clients my way. She also knew her business well and devised the best strategy for me to make big bucks. A mixture of night-time outcalls and day shifts in the rooms, her reasoning for working on-site during the day was because many of her very wealthy clients come during the day; they have wives and can't do nights or outcalls.

I had already done outcalls for Lilith; my favourite was a mate of her partner, Andrew. His mate and I got along so well; he wasn't a phone and extend-by-the-hour kind of guy. He would just book me for the whole evening, and we would party at his penthouse until the sun came up. We did this quite often, and we never ran out of things to discuss; he was a lot of fun, but now it's time for my first-day shift in the rooms. I'm nervous as I haven't massaged sober, and they already have me booked all day, the first being 2 hours with a guy called Ian.

Ian knocks on the door. I open it to greet him, and I'm talking fast; I apologise and tell him I'm a little nervous. He is very kind and offers to sit down and chat before showering. We are chatting, and I find myself hanging off his every word. We are vibing; I have never met anyone like him, and I'm finding myself really attracted to him. I undress and tell him he should take his shower. He comes out of the shower, and his penis is already erect; I haven't even touched him yet, so I can tell he likes me too. I start massaging his back, and he is so into it that it's turning me on. It's time for him to turn over, and I can see his penis is really erect now. I don't usually let clients kiss me but I welcomed his. This is insanity; I have never been so sexually aroused that I almost forget where I am.

I don't know what came over me; I desperately wanted to have sex with this man. We are both so into each other, but neither of us has a condom. I was so embarrassed to call reception to ask; they laughed; they probably thought I had broken my no extras policy in the first booking. This was not an extra; Ian was not paying me for sex. I wanted so badly to have sex with him, and I was not disappointed; the sex was mind-blowing; our sexual attraction was like nothing I had experienced; it was through the roof. Not long after, he wanted me all to himself, asked me to leave work, and offered to pay all my bills. He even paid six months upfront for a lease on a brand-new plush apartment in the Gazebo building in Potts Point.

He told everyone we met in February of 2006, but we had taken an overseas trip together before then. Additionally, he said he was separated from his wife but still lived under the same roof. I believed him, but I also believed him when he said he was 48. In the first few days of Jan 2006, I discovered he was 56, I was 30. We were going on holiday, and I saw his passport. I was annoyed that he had lied, but I was already taken with him, so I boarded the plane for my first overseas trip. Photos were taken in Bangkok on January 16, 2006, during one of our first round-the-world trips together; apart from the date stamps on my computer, I know it was early days because I still had my old teeth. I did get them fixed in Thailand because it was a quarter of the price that I would have paid in Australia, but not on that trip.

Quite a tough life for a girl who only just turned 30, wouldn't you say? All this was so long ago, but the tears still flow as I type. It's hard to re-live; the stories we tell ourselves to cope are much easier versions than the actual truth.

Love, Michelle Ashton

Monday, 26ᵗʰ June 2023

Dear Journal,

Today, I feel so grateful that Adonis came into my life and shed light on what I needed to heal. I would never have dealt with half this stuff; it's not that I didn't want to. I didn't acknowledge it as being an issue. I have so much appreciation; he has changed my whole life; I now have a real one. I was emotionally dead, and I didn't even know it. Apart from the few moments of connection to very few people, I had emotionally checked out. I thought I was living an authentic life before this journey began: that thought makes me laugh no end. I would never have been truly happy, and I would have died with these traumas and wounds.

As if your healing shouldn't be enough of a reward. I get another, my Adonis with a heart of gold; seriously, pinch me. Amongst all this shit, I did something right. I just sent a text message I thought was nice, but I hope that isn't classed as chasing as it's not coming from that needy part of me; it's just pure love.

Just so you know, if you ever need me you are set up to get through my focus status or silent mode. I'm always here for you. Hope you have the most beautiful & relaxing time away.

Love, Michelle Ashton

Tuesday, 27th June 2023

Dear Journal,

I am so tired today; I woke up at three after a bad dream and couldn't get back to sleep. I was living in the townhouse I shared with my ex-husband at 45a Spencer Street in Rose Bay. It was just another usual night of me trying to explain how I felt and him shutting me down. Ian would turn it around by shouting, what about me and how I feel. I was used to never being heard; my feelings were unimportant to him. I lived for years like this and would bury it deep down, but this nightmare sparked something. I was crying like a baby. I honestly thought I had dealt with all the Ian shit. Most nights, he would become a belligerent drunk, and I would move away from him, off the couch, to try to get out of the firing line. I would sit on the floor with my beloved fur baby Pucci, pronounced poo-chi, who would lick mummy's tears. Poor Pooch, what a dysfunctional environment he was living in. Ian's rants often got so bad that I would leave the lounge room altogether and sit in bed, daydreaming about having a place of my own, one where I could live in peace. Even to this day, I am petrified of living with another man. Every single time I have, it has ended badly. I have always been the one to leave and start over every forking time. It's not just the financial costs; the mental and emotional costs are too high.

I have a Motivation app that randomly sends quotes, and just as I was finishing my entry, this one was delivered to my phone.

"If you don't leave your past in your past, it will destroy your future."

Love, Michelle Ashton

Wednesday, 28th June 2023

Dear Journal,

I felt beautiful energy last night. I always wonder if he is trying to connect or if it's his higher self. I know Twin Flames can communicate telepathically. I must say I'm loving this energy lately; apart from my healing tears, there are no tears or sadness about or from him—just a feeling of love. I hope he is having a beautiful, relaxing time away, and I pray this energy is here to stay; it's like I can finally breathe. I still think of him 24/7, but it's not a needy feeling. Have we hit a new place in our journeys? I don't know, but I am hopeful this will last.

I am freezing and just had a random thought. I don't know anyone who can't stand the cold weather as much as me. Since we share a Soul, I wonder if Adonis dislikes it too. I could happily move to a hot climate and never wear a warm jumper again as long as I live. I have Port Douglas in Queensland constantly on the weather app on my phone. I see it daily, but I especially love to imagine being there in the cold winter and on days like today.

- Twin Flame telepathy, quite simply, is telepathic communication between two Twin Flames. Without physical or verbal interaction, they can send and receive information.

Love, Michelle Ashton

Thursday, 29th June 2023

Dear Journal,

I am so tired again today. Journal, you're probably sick of hearing it. I can tell you I'm fed up being and writing it. When I have bad dreams, I acknowledge that these things need healing. I have reached a new place in my journey. I recognise that I am being shown what needs my attention and welcome the signs, no matter how painful. I never thought I would get to a point where I would embrace suffering; I know it's for my highest good. As soon as I release the bad, I make space for the good. It reminds me of the quote, "You can't start the next chapter of your life if you keep re-reading the last one."

Love, Michelle Ashton

Friday, 30th June 2023

Dear Journal,

I was cleaning up and found old financial papers. I realised what a fool I had been. In Ian's handwriting, he had written out everything to be split between us, including the proceeds after paying the mortgage for our home in Rose Bay, a harbourside eastern suburb of Sydney. Ian wanted me to style the house for sale whilst we moved into separate floors of another property. We had agreed to share the home in Birchgrove, an inner city waterfront suburb, for twelve months before going our separate ways. Ian took out the lease in his name, and the rent was to come out of money we had both agreed to put aside. We set up a joint account for the first time in our marriage to cover the costs. I was in the tiny basement of this property that could only fit a double bed and had no heating or air. Ian had the top-floor reverse cycle air-conditioned main bedroom, with a king-sized bed overlooking the harbour bridge and two lovely outdoor terraces.

Looking back, I have no idea why I agreed to this; I just wanted out and anything to help keep the peace. I then had the job of furnishing and styling the two separate homes on a shoestring whilst continuing to work on my start-up. I knew the better I could present the property in Rose Bay, the bigger the return we would receive. It was tough as I could not purchase anything without Ian coming to the store to give his ok. I found it very hard to be creative when I couldn't even buy so much as a picture on my own, not to mention we have entirely different tastes. I would describe Ian's taste as Ralph Lauren on a budget, and mine is more bohemian.

We entered our 2nd lengthy Covid lockdown shortly after both houses were complete. While I was living there, no one visited. It was illegal to do so, not his family, nor mine, no friends. The removalists were the only people ever to step foot on the Birchgrove property. Living together, separated during lockdown with this man, was unbearable; alcohol was the only thing that got me through the days. After we had interest in our Rose Bay property. Ian then waved some paper before me, saying you forgot you signed this, didn't you? It was the prenup I had signed over a decade ago; it was so long ago.

I'm not proud of what came out of my mouth next. I said, "You see you next Tuesday". I called my brother, crying hysterically; I'm going to be destitute at my age. At the time my brother had shares in a law firm and called the managing partner Pierre Safi. He is such a lovely, kind, and caring man. He met with me straight away; I was beside myself; I had been such a good and loyal wife to this man. If he hadn't always taken his children's side, even when they were blatantly disrespectful and rude to me, I would have put up with all his other shit until his last breath. I didn't deserve this treatment. Pierre asked me lots of questions, including where we met. He is the first person I have ever told. Even though it was so long ago, I was still so ashamed; I had guarded that secret for years. He also asked about the lawyer who handled the prenup. Ian's high-profile lawyer, Chris Dimock, drafted it, the same firm that handled two of his three divorces. Ian organised and paid for my lawyer, and I went to sign the prenup. After all this information, Pierre assured me I would not be left destitute after fifteen years together. I returned to Birchgrove and was honest with Ian about what Pierre said.

Ian was very nice, which was great; I don't like fighting and arguing. He said he would pay me a small fraction of what we had previously agreed, if I would sign a binding financial agreement. He also said Pierre would object, but to tell him this is what I wanted. I then called Pierre; as Ian had predicted, he vehemently disagreed. I told Pierre I didn't care about the money, and as long as I had a little, I would be okay. He disagreed; I explained that I pray and meditate daily. I don't want to fight this out; it's not who I am. Please, Pierre, let's finish this so I can live peacefully. I went against my lawyer's advice and signed the binding financial agreement. After this, Ian kicked me out of the house I was expecting to be sharing for 12 months; it had been five, and I was to leave as soon as possible. Luckily, this time, I had somewhere to go. I had purchased a small apartment on the highway in Arncliffe during my drunken lockdown days; it was a stone's throw from Sydney Airport and in a hot spot. A hot spot was an area where the virus was spreading during the Covid-19 pandemic, so the area had different laws and tougher restrictions; it's the same apartment I live in today.

The more documents I read, the angrier I got. The prenup stated it would change if we were to have children. Was that also why he dragged his feet at the start of our marriage? I don't want to believe anyone could be that evil;

it's unfathomable, but he is the world's greediest man. I also threw out my last copies of both our wedding DVDs; we edited the original one. Our wedding was a small ceremony in Thailand with seven guests, including his two children. His daughter was rude to me in her wedding speech on the original DVD; we had 60 copies. We had them made as wedding favours for a party in Australia when we returned from our honeymoon. Even though it was so stressful to get them edited overseas at the last minute, between our wedding and honeymoon, it had to be done. I didn't want our friends and family to think badly of her, so new copies were made.

The realisation of just how much of a doormat I had been has made me want to stand up for myself and have strong boundaries. I want absolutely nothing to do with that man as long as I live. I never want to see his face again. I consigned all the jewellery he had bought me except for two pieces. One was my original wedding ring, which I found such pleasure in throwing in the garbage bin. Another piece is now owned by the jeweller because guess what? I dropped off the three cartier bracelets I wore to be cleaned before going to auction. Cartier informed me one of the screws couldn't be fixed, and they gave me a brand new one. A free $12,000 love bracelet, tell me that wasn't Divinely orchestrated. My gift from the Divine now sits next to my favourite Angel bracelet from Goldmark, and my equally loved crystal Spiritus Stones bracelet; what a perfect trio.

Love, Michelle Ashton

Saturday, 1st July 2023

Dear Journal,

I felt lightheaded this morning; this energy thing is so peculiar. Is it him, is he surfing or some other sport where he is going upside down? Before this journey began, you think nothing of it and sit, while waiting for it to pass. It is so weird to have to second-guess your feelings. I wonder if we could have felt each other before locking eyes? Did he experience head pain whilst I was having brain surgery? I have so many questions about this beautiful and totally bizarre connection.

Love, Michelle Ashton

Sunday, 2nd July 2023

Dear Journal,

I was guided to book this one-day grief yoga retreat with an incredible teacher, Devpreet from, Collective Healing. After taking some of her online Kundalini yoga sessions during the Covid lockdowns, I began to make many positive changes in my life. I am forever grateful for her help. She is an extraordinary Soul who is here to raise the collective consciousness. This retreat is near her hometown on the Central Coast. It's a long drive from my home in Arncliffe, so I got up at 6 a.m. I had no idea why I was going, and then it became so apparent.

We all sat in a circle, Including Devpreet and the lovely registered nurse and counsellor Karen Booth; these are two phenomenal women who also add Gestalt psychotherapists to their resumes. We are instructed to say a few words about why we are here. Everyone takes a turn, all beautiful Souls with one thing in common: each deal with grief; their stories are so sad, and I feel such compassion mixed with guilt. I am guilty because I don't even know why I am here, unlike the others in the circle. Next, we are given coloured pencils and a sheet of paper. We are led in a short meditation, and then we are to draw whatever comes, reminded that we don't have to be artists, just to put pencils to paper. I am astounded at what I have drawn. Looking at me on the paper is the word mother with a cross through it, the words I hate you, you stole this from me, and a beautiful butterfly. I am suddenly aware of why I am here; I need to let go of the grief over not becoming a mother and the resentment I hold towards my ex-husband. I always wonder if he hadn't dragged his feet earlier in our marriage, if my dream to become a mother would have been a reality. The truth is, I will never know if I would have been lucky enough to have a little mini-me call me Mum. I will never be called that name, but it is one I so desperately wanted.

By the time this loving and supportive retreat came to a close, many tears have been shed between us. I make the long drive home, still in shock at today's events. I didn't see this coming; that's precisely how my healing journey unfolds. If I feel guided towards something, there is a reason.

I have finally learned to listen to my intuition. When I arrived home, I burned my drawing, a picture of Ian and me, and our marriage certificate. I feel so good. Healing is tough, but your natural high afterwards is worth every tear.

Love, Michelle Ashton

Monday, 3rd July 2023

Dear Journal,

Even though it wasn't ideal for me to have a healing session on a Monday, I had to squeeze one in where I could. I was busy on the weekend. On Saturday, I saw a friend for her birthday and then visited my brother and my beautiful niece and nephew. My Angelic niece's 7th birthday is on Friday. My brother only has them part-time, and it's hard for him the other times; he misses them so much. Without a doubt, I'm sure this contributes to his destructive behaviour. Don't get me wrong, I have seen him partying for as long as I can remember. However, since his divorce and not being able to be with the kids full-time, I have seen his crazy lifestyle escalate to the point that it scares me. He is such a good dad; I am so proud of that. Seeing him in action is really something. Like our dad, he is super fun, but unlike our father, he is never irresponsible when the kids are around. They are his number one priority; it's just beautiful to watch. I admire his absolute dedication to their upbringing. He is not only fun, but he also teaches them things, including manners, which they sometimes don't like, ha. I'm sure they will appreciate it in the future.

Just quietly, I love visiting when the kids are there; not only do I get to see my niece and nephew, who I could not love anymore if I tried, they are such characters. My niece is a replica of my brother; she is such a caring little girl, empathetic, sweet-natured, and very intelligent. She will have the world at her feet that one. My nephew is also sweet-natured; he loves with every fibre in his being and has a smile that could light up a room. This one has my brother's cheekiness, which is funny to watch. He is such a determined little boy, for only three and a half years old, apart from the joy I receive from spending time with my favourite kids in the world. I get to see my brother, the real Seb; it warms my heart to see and spend time with him, not the shadow of himself that I know when the kids aren't around.

That was my Saturday; I try to spend as much time as possible with them, when they are with my brother. Seb and I being so alike means I can see parts of myself in their sweet little faces; my niece has my dark brown eyes, and my nephew Duchenne smiles like I do. It's so adorable and totally foreign to me; I have never experienced this beautiful phenomenon without having kids of my own. I think you may have some understanding of the love and pride I have for these two incredible humans. There are no words to express the amount of my love, so I'll leave it at that.

Now Sunday, I already journalled about that day, so that brings me to today, that's why I saw Reiki Angel on a Monday. She is so intuitive; she is in a league of her own. Without knowing much, she tells me mother issues have arisen for me, and it's heavily blocked. Really, I think to myself, why does this not surprise me? I don't think my mum would be winning mother of the year, that's for sure. I wonder if Adonis also has mother issues; some Twin Flames have similar backgrounds. Oh, my bloody gosh. If this is true, my heart goes out to him like never before.

Love, Michelle Ashton

Tuesday, 4th July 2023

Dear Journal,

I made myself sad today with my thoughts. I imagined how beautiful it would be to spend the night with Adonis, and the first thing I saw in the morning was his perfect face. What a magical start to the day. I love him so much. I had never known a love like this existed. I want to tell him, Adonis, I love you, and I've never felt like this. You are a gift from God; Heaven really is on earth. Then, it was back to reality; that was the sad part.

Love, Michelle Ashton

Wednesday, 5th July 2023

Dear Journal,

I called Salma and said "I have something exciting to tell you." She replied, "Get out of here, Adonis contacted you." I laughed and said no, I wouldn't just say it like that, In a normal voice. I would scream so loud that I wouldn't have to use the phone. They would hear me in Timbuktu.

Love, Michelle Ashton

Thursday, 6th July 2023

Dear Journal,

It's just another day of being tired, laughing one minute and then crying the next. I would love to know what emotions are his. I don't understand why we can't have a conversation; other Twin Flames in separation do. It's tough going through all this alone. I would understand if he needs time; I do. I have a path I need to walk alone on for a little while. I had never envisioned a future with anyone until he came along. He changed my view on everything, but I would still need to take things slow. This journey has been a whirlwind, to say the least; I need to catch my breath.

Love, Michelle Ashton

Friday, 7th July 2023

Dear Journal,

This morning was shit, excuse my French. Journal, you know me very well by now to notice that I say the odd swear word here and there. As a bogan Aussie, it might very well be in my blood. That shouldn't define me.

Back to this morning, I am still not sleeping well, and I was up early to complete my One Kiss work before heading off to see my beautiful Freida. The car has had GPS issues; it started working again, so I cancelled the long-awaited service appointment. I jump in to realise it's again happening. I don't know where I'm going. I stopped to buy a phone dash holder to use Google Maps, but now it keeps falling off. I need to decide if I should let the phone fall and possibly break, which would be super annoying and inconvenient as I need it for work, not to mention it would cost money that I don't have to fix it, or if I should catch the phone. I could lose five demerit points, which would cost more money for a fine and affect my earning ability, as I need my driver's licence for work. Listen to me, seriously, what a winger. I've just had it; I think sleep deprivation is taking a toll. I'm tired and so emotional. I was enjoying my lunch, a veggie bowl from Guzman and Gomez, and out of nowhere, the tears started again. I've decided most men are see you next Tuesday's. I went from a shifty marriage where my ex didn't give a flying fork about me or my welfare. Now, I find myself in this situation where another one doesn't give a fork. Why did this journey have me open my heart to love again, to sit around waiting for someone to become a decent human being? I was listening to a podcast last night about the Divine feminine having to turn their love for the other on themselves. That's exactly what I need to do. I thought this would be the most magical connection ever; yeah, right. I'm sitting in my car crying my eyes out like I'm a five-year-old. I need to get a grip; I'm waiting on someone I don't even know who is coming. Seriously WTF. I know I need to stay positive, so I am enjoying the sunshine coming through the car window. There's something to be grateful for.

Love, Michelle Ashton

Saturday, 8th July 2023

Dear Journal,

I honestly don't think I go a day without tears or a moment without thinking of him. Will I ever be able to lead an everyday life again? What has this man done to me? Am I condemned to live my life in tears, pain and longing? Will I ever be happy and find a way out of this mental prison? Every time I long for him, it energetically repels him. Logically, I know this, but I can't stop; I love and miss him so much. I keep saying I need to put that love on myself, but I want to give it to him—no wonder he wants nothing to do with me. I'm obsessed; I would give anything to spend time with him and try to make him happy. His happiness would be my happiness. I don't know what to do anymore.

I can't see a way out. He is the only one for me. I would never need a celebrity hall pass. What do you call it when a couple have a pact that if either meets their crush and has the chance to spend the night with them, they have the go-ahead? I don't know what it's called, because I don't need it. Adonis is mine. He is the ultimate man for me. If I ever have the opportunity to love him, he will never want to let me go.

Love, Michelle Ashton

Sunday, 9th July 2023

Dear Journal,

Adonis has given me the gift of life, and now I have to find a way to give myself the gift of freedom. I just have to find a way. It's so consuming, all day, every day, I can't even go to sleep without dreaming about him. I've said before that I think of this man as much as I breathe. Twin Flame chasers have it so challenging, and it may be even harder for me as I live and mostly work alone. I can't change my circumstances, so please, God, help me find a way. I can't go on like this. Please help me, I beg of you. For months now, I've been totally in love with him. I know his Soul; he is just so perfect, such a beautiful man, and that's just the inside; look at the outside; it should be forking illegal to be that hot.

Love, Michelle Ashton

Monday, 10th July 2023

Dear Journal,

This evening I decided to watch a programme. I rarely watch anything. I always listen to music, but sometimes I indulge in Gaia. I enjoy Spiritual-type shows; tonight, I watched one about love, and someone talked about how being a mother is the best gift ever. I cry so much; that ship has sailed. The only saving grace is that if I were lucky enough to have been blessed, knowing myself, I would never have left. I may have been with fork-head until the end of time. I can't imagine ever putting my needs above theirs. This is mean what I'm about to say, but since we have no secrets in the journal, here goes. I thought about how repulsed my Soul must have been while I was with Ian. I can't stop crying; I don't know how to forgive myself. No one would ever understand how much I loved that man. What was wrong with me? He is older than my father; I was one very broken girl. Now that I see Souls, I look at our pictures, and he is so ugly to me that I can't find one redeeming quality. I am crying so hard, and then I hear it's not your fault; you didn't know any better. Great advice; now for some self-empathy.

Love, Michelle Ashton

Tuesday, 11th July 2023

Dear Journal,

I had an appointment with the Twin Flame reader today; as always, I wanted to see if he was okay. He is more than ok; he might be on a dating app. What changed in Thailand? So much for my newfound confidence in our connection. I've absolutely had it with this roller coaster. How does one trust the process, thinking about their Divine counterpart sharing their body with another? I can hardly journal through my tears; it's too painful of a thought. It is a different kettle of fish for Twin Flame runners. I'm not going to have any more Twin Flame readings; I don't want to know. When I prayed this morning, I asked for the next steps in this journey to be shown to me. Is this it? Is this my Karma for checking up and not surrendering? I hear you loud and clear, Divine.

Now, to try to erase the thought of Adonis with some skank. I apologise for my harsh words, whoever you are. I'm sure you're not a skank; it's just that you can find someone else. Not me; this man has my heart and Soul for Eternity.

Love, Michelle Ashton

Wednesday, 12th July 2023

Dear Journal,

It's almost 12 weeks since the realisation of my Spiritual awakening. I must say it feels like a bloody lifetime. My feelings for this beautiful man grow stronger and stronger. It's unbelievable that you can feel this way for another person. Even if he turns up tomorrow, I need to take things slowly; the ghosting and separation have been too much. I don't want either of us getting freaked out and running again. Unless we are both healed, we will continue to trigger each other. If we can't understand and accept that we are just showing one another what needs to be worked on to overcome, we will blame the other person and run from them instead of looking within. Even if I was the runner, as I have read, you can switch roles so each Twin Flame can experience running and chasing. Understanding the pain, I have gone through as a chaser. I couldn't cope knowing I was inflicting this pain onto another, let alone, my perfect Adonis, who I love with all my heart. Maybe we could be friends and build on that. I don't know the answer; I've never gotten to know someone I'm already in love with. I know that I could not endure separation again. This connection is like no other; we can't fork it up.

Love, Michelle Ashton

Thursday, 13th July 2023

Dear Journal,

    I was singing at the top of my lungs, dancing, and having fun, and then I burst into tears when I realised that I was enjoying myself so much, completely sober. Then I thought, I haven't taken drugs for a while. The last time was coke in mid-May, and I only did a little to join in; I was home at 11.30 pm. The time before that was the Red Hot Chill Peppers concert in early Feb when I was completely smashed out of my mind on ecstasy. I don't need drugs to have fun; what an epiphany. After 30+ years of taking drugs, I now realise I don't need them to have fun.
    Oh my goodness, seriously, all these years. I wonder what else this journey has in store for me. Wow, I'm in such awe of how magical the Universe is. I will be conscious to make an effort to repay wherever I can, giving back to help people and the planet. I will do everything I can to help; how do you repay the gift of life? I will start with my brother. I love him so much that I decided to drop back all supplies, including my infamous car key. This car key has a waterproof hidden compartment to store my drugs; I will not need it. I do this so Seb realises I am serious. Instead of shoving my newfound wisdom down his throat, I will lead by example, showing him that you don't need drugs to have fun—something I should have done years ago.

Love, Michelle Ashton

Friday, 14th July 2023

Dear Journal,

This afternoon, I got to pick up my beautiful niece and nephew. It is always a long drive from Bondi Junction to Cronulla, but it is even longer when you have such precious cargo on board. My nephew requested that we play Jingle Bells, which we sang at the top of our lungs with the car windows open—not once but thrice in the middle of July. Ha, kids crack me up. Then it was my niece's turn to choose; it seems like her Tay Tay days are behind her; she decided on Back In Black by ACDC, and now we are talking. Not long after, my nephew showed me what he thought about Aunty Shelly's driving. Puke, barf, chunder, whatever you wish to call it everywhere, poor darling, I thought I was a good driver.

Later that evening, back at home alone, my mind is again on Adonis. Why did God have to make him so perfect? It makes it awful hard to even think about entertaining another. I'll say it repeatedly: I will never get tired of telling the world what a special Soul he is—wrapped in the absolute hottest package. Hands down, that man is a 10 out of 10. My mind then goes to all Twin Flames, trying to wrap my head around runners. Why on Earth would anyone run from unconditional love? I thought this journey was crazy; that's the most insane part.

Love, Michelle Ashton

Saturday, 15th July 2023

Dear Journal,

I awoke so tired this morning. I am concerned for Adonis, as I'm pretty sure this is not my energy. I texted him out of concern, not for my benefit; it was coming from a place of pure love. I want him to know I am always here for him. It's hard for me, too, and I keep most things to myself. It would be nice to share the burden, but I have no control. However, I am beyond blessed to have my friend Salma in my corner; she is the only one who knows I'm on this crazy and magical journey. She is so happy for me and for all the changes I have made along the way. There is only one change she isn't sure about—the vegan lifestyle, as we love to eat together.

We used to make cabanossi pizzas after school at her place. I love that she loves food as much as I do. Our motto is, why wait for the next lifetime to indulge? I explained to her that eating an animal is like a human eating a human. It's forking repulsive. I will never be a person who protests against people living their lives the way they choose. I have lived a very colourful life and would never judge another Soul. It has never been my style; now, it is even less. Personally, I have complete love and compassion for every living thing on our incredible planet, humans and animals alike.

Love, Michelle Ashton

Sunday, 16th July 2023

Dear Journal,

I am so much kinder to myself now. Today, I went to a Buddhist workshop; I love these: I may have mentioned before that I hang off every word. Afterwards, I drove to Clovelly Beach, grabbed some takeaway, and ate in the car overlooking the water. It's raining, but it's nice to know the trees are getting a drink, and it makes such a beautiful sound. Looking at the sea, I'm deep in thought. I have been so focused on my feelings that I am not sure if, even for a minute, I had thought about how Adonis might feel. Does he want to reach out but is terrified that I don't feel the same? Does he think I'm not the girl for him and feels trapped? Is he scared to embark on his healing journey?

These are just a few of the many unanswered questions. I have to find a way to be okay with maybe never finding the answers. This makes me cry; no one would ever know what a big softie I am. I don't show anyone this side of me because I've always had to be tough. Appearing weak in this dog-eat-dog world is a liability. This thought makes me cry even more; how sad is it that we live in a society where we don't feel safe enough to be ourselves? Imagine we all lived in a world where we not only felt safe enough to be ourselves, but it was celebrated. This thought makes me want to do a Tom Cruise couch jump, but multiplied by infinity.

Love, Michelle Ashton

Monday, 17th July 2023

Dear Journal,

What a weird dream I had; it was strangely beautiful. Adonis called me on my mobile. I have no idea where I was, but for some reason, Ian was there. Adonis didn't say a word; I only could hear him breathing on the other end of the phone. In the background, Ian was banging around, making so much noise, trying to distract me. I just zoned him out, concentrated on my Adonis, and the next minute Ian was gone. No words were spoken between us, but it was such a special moment; hearing this man breathe is the best sound in the world—such a lovely start to my week.

At the end of my day, still thinking of Adonis, I send him another text message.

Hi beautiful, I really hope you're doing well? I really do

I honestly never know if I should reach out or not. I always find it so hard to know what to say & im normally not one to be lost for words

It is the hardest situation I've ever been in, in my entire life. I have so much love & compassion for you that I only want the absolute best for you, whatever that means for YOU. it's a real tricky spot for me to be in, I just wish you would trust me enough to reach out. Absolutely no pressure, no headache, no demands. I seriously only want you to be happy, gosh I wish you really understood that. I've hit a point in this journey, that I tear up just writing this, wanting you to understand that, I only want you to be happy. You might not understand that now, maybe down the track you will, who knows, I just had to put it in words, you're too special to me. Hope you get a good night sleep x

I always hope that one of these days, I get a reply.

Love, Michelle Ashton

Tuesday, 18th July 2023

Dear Journal,

Today, I am reflecting on how much kinder I am to myself and how happy I am that I have waffled on with my feelings, even the not-so-pretty ones. It's a great reminder of how far I've come. I am very proud of myself; it hasn't been easy. I only work two jobs now. My passion, One Kiss, and NDIS work with beautiful Freida. I no longer drive for Uber; I allow myself time to rest. The work schedule I was keeping, I wouldn't expect anyone to do, let alone someone I love. I am so grateful that I can see that now. I no longer live in survival mode. In this present moment, I'm okay. I have stopped living in fear of the future. I could die tomorrow; why die all stressed? Life is too short.

Love, Michelle Ashton

Wednesday, 19th July 2023

Dear Journal,

I woke up feeling great. I love today's energy. I go about my day invigorated and then check my One Kiss Facebook. Ian liked one of my posts. Why? I blocked him everywhere; I don't often use Facebook, and I didn't think about it. I immediately block him and cower in the corner. Until I started healing, I never realised how badly I was treated. That narcissist manipulated me for 15 years. It wasn't just the big things; it was everything. I couldn't do a thing right in his eyes, literally a thing. There is a water line on the Aarke soda stream bottle; every time I filled it, it was either too little or too much. I can't believe I not only put up with all his shit but loved him with all my heart. The thought makes me sick to my stomach. Now, he wouldn't even get a hello on the street, and I am nice to everyone. No wonder I am petrified of living with a man. How will I ever learn to trust another?

Love, Michelle Ashton

Thursday, 20th July 2023

Dear Journal,

What a day. I always do whatever I'm guided, regardless of my thoughts. I trust the Divine and just go with it. This healing appointment was definitely outside the box, with holistic pelvic care at Natural Beginnings in Caringbah South. I was guided to the very kind and caring Virginia a few weeks back. I booked the recommended three appointments, and today was my first. We sat down to have a chat. Virginia is open-minded and didn't bat an eyelid when I told her I have been on a Spiritual journey. I was guided to her, and I don't know why. She also must be open to communication from the Divine, as most people look at you like you are completely nuts; this reassures me that I am here for a reason, and Virginia is the woman to help me find out.

Talk about trusting the Divine; this was on another level. Virginia had gloves on, fingers inside, pressing against different pelvic spots, explaining that we can hold a lot of emotions in this area, and if the tears flow, let them embrace the emotional release. I was totally fine; it felt like a massage for your hoo-ha until one spot was pressed, and tears streamed down my face. Virginia asked if I had any memories. No, nothing, I'm just so emotional. The appointment was over; I got into the car and cried all the way home. WTF was that all about? What did she press on? I have no idea, but I can assure you it certainly wasn't my G spot.

Love, Michelle Ashton

Friday, 21st July 2023

Dear Journal,

Last night, I dreamt of Adonis, but what's new? Well, this is. I told him that I loved him. I woke up thinking how beautiful it was, and then I started to cry. What if I never get the chance to tell him? I can only hope that one day, he will know just how deep my feelings are and how grateful I am that he came into my life. I am in a good place now. I still heal, but it's not bedridden healing. When it comes up, I deal with it and move on. I've never had calmness like this; it's incredible. Even traffic doesn't bother me. I love this sweet spot.

Love, Michelle Ashton

Saturday, 22nd July 2023

Dear Journal,

Let's start with last night. I sent this text to Adonis. I am curious to find out so many things. Maybe one day, he will reach out.

How are you? I pray you're well beautiful.

I have so many questions, gosh I wish I could get answers!

I have had so many changes over the last months, I am so f...ing proud of myself, I love this chick

This latest one is something that I wonder where this is coming from. I have a complete fascination with the planet. I google, I watch docs. I look for every product that's better for the environment. I really wonder if it's coming from you or it's normal with ascending.

My best mate Salma knows about my complete fascination & asked if you were into that stuff & im like I dunno, she all so asked if you were vegetarian as she is in shock about that change & im also like I dunno. Maybe I'll ask my Reike Angel tomorrow about the planet ascending stuff.

I really wish you would reach out at some point, now this is a magical journey for months I was in h.. OMG, seriously Beyond. I'm proud, I'm still here to text you, so hard. I didn't even realise how strong I was... when I think about how bad it was. I pray it isn't so bad for you, actually I pray for that everyday.

Anyhow, I just have so many questions that I never get answers to. I don't think it's normal for complete no contact, I don't know what your reasoning is for seeing & not replying. I just have to trust you that you have a good reason & trust your process too.

Sending so much love & don't forget I'm always here :-)

Now, this morning, back to this unbelievable, beautiful moment. I was meditating, just as I have for years, and out of nowhere, I started to chant, I am one with the Universe, over and over and over. Then I heard, I give you the gift of compassion. This journey is seriously magical; I am so blessed; no words can express my gratitude.

Love, Michelle Ashton

Sunday, 23rd July 2023

Dear Journal,

I have a set of goals written on my bedroom mirror. Last night, I ticked off the first. I drank red wine, got some liquid courage and messaged. I've been wanting to have the guts to say this for ages.

I hope your well babes?

F... this...

I have goals written down & my number 1 is to tell Adonis I love him..

So here goes, I love you. I said it not how I would have liked to have said it but I don't get any other chance. I love you.

Good night beautiful x

Now, to achieve the next 10

1. ~~Tell Adonis I Love him~~
2. Be in a position to triple I=Change donations & partner with Ecolgi (to plant one tree per sale)
3. Pay Seb back
4. Have an office with staff
5. Buy a humble home by the beach (add solar panels, have a compost, filtered water taps etc)
6. Have a beloved fur baby
7. Buy an electric car
8. Always be conscious of our planet (personally and for One Kiss)
9. Be so happy, healthy & content
10. Travel
11. Retire somewhere hot (Port Douglas, Bali, Thailand)

Love, Michelle Ashton

Monday, 24th July 2023

Dear Journal,

I had what I thought was a sexy dream about him last night, but I swear I was only half asleep. It seemed so real. I loved it. Then it was morning and back to reality.

Every day, I pray for a sign of the next steps forward, as I can't continue living on this roller coaster. I start to feel better, then boom. I've done so much work to get to this place, but still, I haven't heard one peep. Is it just a chaser's role to think about them non-stop? Why would God do this? I don't know what else I can do. Give me a sign PLEASE, I beg of you. This is strength on another level. I wish I could stay in bed; it's a good thing I don't have time; I'd probably cry all day.

Love, Michelle Ashton

Tuesday, 25th July 2023

Dear Journal,

Again, last night. I wonder where all these sexy dreams come from. Don't get me wrong, I welcome them, but I hope my neighbours don't hear, ha. He is one passionate man if the dreams are anything to go by. Woah!

Love, Michelle Ashton

Wednesday, 26th July 2023

Dear Journal,

I love being guided. I am always pushed to do things that are good for me. Instead of sitting at my desk for hours on end, I now set alarms at intervals to go for a short walk and stretch my legs. I am on my walk around my building, and I am guided to run. I am scared; the last time I ran was before my brain surgery in 2011. On the grass, I ran. I lasted ten seconds before feeling dizzy and off balance, but I did it. Happy tears are streaming down my face. My left-hand holds my cereal bowl, and I ran for a little. What's next, Divine? Bring it on!

Love, Michelle Ashton

Thursday, 27th July 2023

Dear Journal,

This morning, I went to my first Pilates session in forever. I was trying to think back to my last class. I don't think I've been all year. Before this journey began, I was going three to four times a week. These last months have been a challenge, to say the least. Then, it was just a regular workday but filled with breaks like regular folk. I discovered that my building has a little bench in a grassed area. I try to get some sunshine during my lunch hour on days like today. That's something new. I had never allowed myself lunch breaks before. I would spend five minutes eating at my desk and then move on to the next task. I love my new and improved life, but then the evening comes; they are the hardest.

Tonight, I tried to call Adonis; I have no idea why this made me want to contact him. I was watching a planet documentary when I started laughing uncontrollably. It's a really sweet gesture that the penguins make, and I shouldn't make fun. He hands her a stone when the male wants to court a female. I suppose it's just like humans giving an engagement ring. The more I think about it, the more I love the penguin's idea; it's perfect. I prefer a stone over a diamond; it's more bohemian, just my style. Guess what? I found I was still blocked; I was annoyed just a tad! I send a text. I hope he has an Android phone and will someday locate my message and enjoy the read.

Hi, that was the first time in forever I actually tried to call you. I found something really funny & for some silly reason. I just thought I wanted to wave the white flag & say hi. I find you still you have me blocked. Seriously it's almost 7 months later since we hung out/ really hung out if you know what I mean. WTF Noah, if you ever even want to hang out again in the future, you aren't taking the right steps? You might have to re think your strategy if it's ever something you think you might want, Just think about how you would react with your current strategy & viola there is your answer, or if never seeing me again is what you want then all good, you're doing perfectly! I'm sorry to be a hard arse I'm just super frustrated here, I simply can't keep banging my head against a wall. I told you how I feel & nothing, zero, Zilch it's not really the warmest fuzziest feeling babe. I have dreams that are so real, I still don't sleep well. You know exactly what's going on by now. You could just text back & say I need a month, 6, a year I'm not even sure if it's something that I ever want or I don't know even know what to say or simply the same again "I'm just not into you that way" Omg I'm sorry for that one, that was mean, I'm just hurt once again. Hope you get a good night sleep :-)

A little time passed, and I'm really pissed off now. I sent another message, but he got a taste of his own medicine this time. Immediately after, I block him back.

I need to have some control in my life too, it's not all about you. Omg that reminds me of what you text me before you blocked me. Great minds think alike hey! So WOW here you go it took me almost 7 months to do this. I love you & you don't give 2 shits.

I know where you work & where you live & I have left you alone to do what you had to do for months & months. I work from home & you don't know what apartment number I am so Goodluck trying to find me & now the only connection you have to me "phone" you're blocked too. I really love you, it's so sad. you are the silliest sod right now, enjoy life & whatever her name is!

Finally, it took me months to get here. My heart hurts, but I am so proud that I finally stood up for myself. What's next? Go Shell.

Love, Michelle Ashton

Friday, 28th July 2023

Dear Journal,

I thought I would sleep well; it was the worst in forever. I had vivid dreams all night long, but I was standing up for myself. I am even getting stronger in dreamland; yay! It feels good not to wait and wonder if he will be courageous enough to reach out. I need a decent night's sleep; I may need to take Valium. That disturbs me; I hate taking anything now. I have cut out so many meds. It would be a last resort, how times have changed.

Love, Michelle Ashton

Saturday, 29th July 2023

Dear Journal,

I slept so well last night. My Friday night was perfect. I had my favourite local Thai takeaway. This Thai restaurant has the best food I have tasted outside of Thailand. I am blessed that Land Thai kitchen is on my doorstep. I devoured a tofu, veggie, chilli basil stir-fry and washed it down with a couple of gluten-free beers. I applied a face mask and enjoyed a candle-lit bath while jazz-rock covers played in the background. I couldn't feel his energy last night and again today. Maybe the Divine has given me a break; it has happened before.

Once, I remember having a massive breakdown, crying for about 6 hours straight. Another time, I had a panic attack and such bad anxiety that I couldn't get out of my car. I had to give myself a pep talk to get out, up my lift and into my apartment, where I sat on the floor and sobbed uncontrollably. On both occasions afterwards, I couldn't feel him. Maybe they sense you need a break, or he could be with someone. If it's the latter, thank you Divine, I don't want to feel that.

In the bath last night, I thought I'm going to be forty-eight soon. I want to find someone I can still laugh with when I'm ninety. Before Adonis came along, that was the last thing on my mind; now, I'm open to finding love again. I don't want to mess around with anyone just for fun and waste my time and theirs. I can't imagine seeing anyone hold a candle to Adonis, but as long as they are kind, respectful and loyal to me, I will treat them like a king.

Love, Michelle Ashton

Sunday, 30th July 2023

Dear Journal,

Driving back from dinner with my brother last night, I cried all the way home. I casually asked if Noah had been in contact since returning from Thailand. Seb said "No, that's a bit weird." I shrugged and said "maybe he is seeing someone." The insecure me wondered if he had seen me lately and thought, ew. I no longer colour my hair; the eyelash extensions, collagen and Botox injections are a thing of the past. I rarely wear makeup or blow-dry my hair. My tummy isn't flat anymore, and I've put on weight. This is me; it makes me sad to think that maybe he is just as superficial as most men I've met. Being my Twin Flame, I expected him to be the same as me; I don't judge anyone. I have concluded that how we look is just a way of being recognised. If people want to spend hours on the way they wish to be identified, go for it. Right now, I'm comfortable the way I am, and if that changes in the future, whatever. We all need to stop judging and let each other be.

Anyhow enough, I have work to do. I don't usually work on weekends now, but my beautiful Kon needs me to look at something. Konstantina Mittas I met through a friend; she is unbelievably talented. I am still in disbelief that someone of her calibre took me and my little label under her wing. I will be forever grateful, so I will try to briefly forget about Adonis and reply to her email.

Love, Michelle Ashton

Monday, 31st July 2023

Dear Journal,

Is Adonis happy, and are we mirroring each other? I'm ecstatic; I can't stop smiling; it's beautiful. The only time I frowned, which I can do now, by the way. Anyone who has had Botox injections would understand. It was when I watched David Attenborough: A Life on Our Planet and was so disturbed. I think sometimes the human race can either be: a, not aware, or b, selfish, or c, a bit of both. Seriously, how hard is it to make a few tiny changes? If we all did, imagine the impact. Unfortunately, some of us only notice when it affects us, like Covid. At least with that, we could make changes after the fact. What happens when we realise that we have killed our planet? What then? Seriously people? Please don't wait until it's too late or think it's not your problem; it's the next generation. We should be ashamed of ourselves. I am so glad I woke up to some issues I could address. One person isn't going to change the planet, but as a collective, the power to make profound change is within reach; it really is.

Love, Michelle Ashton

Tuesday, 1st August 2023

Dear Journal,

Something has changed. I am always so grateful for all the good, but this is on another level. I am so happy, and I feel like I'm starting to get my life back. I don't want all of it back in any way. I want to mix this powerful woman I have become with the happy-go-lucky Shell. Watch out world. I wonder if Adonis is happy too. I pray for that every day. If I had only one wish in this lifetime, it would be for his happiness.

Love, Michelle Ashton

Wednesday, 2nd August 2023

Dear Journal,

When will this end? I had two days of bliss, and now boom, tears again. I shouldn't complain; I am blessed to be guided to the shadows that need my attention. This is something I completely disregarded. I have been so mean to myself sexually. I have put others' needs above my own for years. Not one person knows the depths of these scars. I never wanted to embarrass my ex-husband. I covered for him and told my close friends, yes, he was older, but a bit of Viagra did the trick. That wasn't the case. He couldn't get it up, even with the meds. I hadn't had sex for years. I'm not sure if it was my brain surgery that turned him off or the affair that deep down I know he had but would never admit to. They were both around the same time; that's when my sex life ended at 36 years old, and I stayed faithful to that man. I was so horny that I asked if I could have sex with another, and it wouldn't be anything but sex, that I loved him. Ian was so angry at my suggestion that I never brought it up again. What was good for the goose wasn't good for the gander. I have seen Ian have sex with so many other women. I honestly couldn't count how many. I loved him, and he knew exactly what he was doing. It makes me sick. At one stage, we lived in a penthouse in Darlinghurst, an inner-city eastern suburb. This was the only time he would pay for the drugs when he called escorts from the local brothel. Most of the time, it was different girls, but sometimes, he would get keen on them, and they would keep coming back until he got bored and moved on. What the fork was wrong with me? How did I not see? He was using drugs to control me. Who wants to watch their fiancé or husband sleeping with other women?

Fast forward to me being single, divorced and able to have sex freely; what have I done? It had been so long that I was extremely nervous, so I toyed with the idea of hiring a male escort, a friend of mine, Lilith, had recommended, but I ultimately chickened out. Then Adonis came along and seemed so kind; I didn't expect only to have sex once and be thrown into this crazy journey. It's healthy to have sex; it's natural. I have put my needs aside for so many years now. I'm not ancient, for fork's sake. I need to start living again; I'm 47, I am not dead.

* Psychiatrist, Psychotherapist, and Psychologist Carl Jung first coined the term "The shadow." What I understand is that it's our dark, repressed wounds, traumas, fears, resentments, and emotions—the things hidden in our unconscious mind because they're too painful. No one wants to confront their darker side, so shadows are simply self-protection mechanisms.

Love, Michelle Ashton

Thursday, 3rd August 2023

Dear Journal,

I'm in the best mood today. I am guided and loving every minute. I went to my Pilates class and asked some regulars if they knew of any nice walks nearby. One of the lovely girls suggested the Bay Walk. I hadn't been down to the beach at Brighton-Le-Sands since I moved to Arncliffe. I used to love the beach but got used to not going since Ian didn't. I moved in a while ago and was so busy dealing with the aftermath of my marriage breakdown that I locked myself away, rarely going out. I got down to the beach and cried tears of joy. I thank my guides. I am so grateful to remember how much I love the beach and what it's like to live my life, not someone else's. At this moment, I make a promise to myself never to allow that to happen again. I will live authentically for the rest of my life. I just remembered something else that was exciting, too. I'm pumped; I have event tickets next Friday for Awakened Life, which is being held by the one and only Deepak Chopra. I am slightly obsessed with this beautiful, intelligent Soul; I would love to share his insights with Adonis, so I unblock and send him a message.

This is a very hard text for me to write. I 100% now know that you need to do your healing in your time. I don't think as much, as I thought I knew before. I ever really grasped the concept but There is a catch, I do have a date as I have 2 tickets that are next Fri, so I have to ask as I think it would be so good for you as well.

If I don't hear from you before tomo night I will ask my girlfriend Salma as I think she would enjoy too.

I really think it would be good for you but I totally understand if you don't even want to hang as a friend, you could give yourself one night off & go back to your healing & not hear from me. You honestly don't know this person that I am now. I am still getting to know her too, she is very chilled, loves life & is a pretty cool chick. I love her. anyhow you do you babe & if you think you are ready for a night off, nothing serious just come as a mate & go back to hibernating. I get it, I've done it for months, believe me. Just text back I'm in. You don't need to stress about anything that has happened in the past, It doesn't matter. Seriously please believe me, no explanation needed. Im in is all you need to say & I'll send you the deets & meet you there :-)

Gosh, I hope he has unblocked me and replies. I can't think of anyone better to get some awakening tips from than my favourite Spiritual Guru. How blessed are we that he is making his way down under? Seriously, pinch me.

Love, Michelle Ashton

Friday, 4th August 2023

Dear Journal,

Life is bloody good. It's great to be alive, mate! This morning, I decided to bugger the gym altogether and head down to the beach. I had a lovely walk, and then, instead of meditating on my cushion inside my bedroom. I decided to sit on the sand and meditate. It was sheer Heaven to hear the seagulls. Unfortunately there were no waves that would have topped it off, but I was so grateful all the same. I then went to the Kiosk and had a yummy granola and fruit bowl in the sun; what a beautiful spot it is down there. I had no phone; I just took in the stunning scenery—the water and birds- what a moment. I can't wait to go back.

I headed downstairs to my storage container to grab my Buddha when I got home. I wanted to put it beside my yoga mat. I think it's the first time I noticed how little I had from all the homes I lived in throughout my marriage.

Everything in my apartment is new. I had to buy a fridge, washer, dryer, kitchen appliances, plates, cutlery, bedding, towels, and everything else. WTF? Ian has a whole house, plus two storage containers full of furniture and bits; he has so much that he has itemised lists. Meanwhile, I have four pictures my family is in, an antique vase, and a lamp we were given as a wedding present. Whilst I was down there, I did call him a greedy see you next Tuesday. I don't feel bad; he is one. I decided I didn't want the bloody lamp; I would leave it downstairs at the main entrance for someone else to enjoy. I walked back with the box, and as soon as I looked down at his handwriting, it said Duffell; the box fell and smashed. I just cracked up; that's what my Soul thought, ha.

That wasn't the only funny thing that happened today. I was eating my lunch, and my bra felt tight. I was at home, so I decided to take it off and thought, why are bras always so uncomfortable? And then I heard, yeah, get your tits out.

It made me laugh hard until I started dying from embarrassment, wondering if and what was being said to him. It's not surprising they say Twin Flames have no secrets.

Love, Michelle Ashton

Saturday, 5th August 2023

Dear Journal,

I now question everything I do and buy. Like most people, I have been using some of the same products for years without a second thought. You name it: prescription meds, vitamins, foods, products, etc. I now try to make the best choices for the planet. I can't work out a better option for some products, like my single-use eye drops. Years back, an eye professor discovered a scar on my left pupil. Ian told the doctor it must have been from the brain surgery. He noticed that since then, I have not closed my eyes fully when sleeping, which he had never told me before this appointment. The eye professor then suggested dry eyes might have caused the scar if I'm not closing them at night, and I should lubricate them every day. Plastic is so bad for the environment, so I have stopped using two vials per day and instead use one. That's a saving of 365 vials being disposed of each year. Every bit counts, and so far, I see no difference, ha.

I also took myself to the movies today. I can't remember the last time I asked myself what I felt like doing today. Off to Randwick Ritz, I went. I love this old-school heritage-listed cinema. I had the best day until I called my brother. His partying is out of control. It's killing me to watch him throwing his life away. I have so much on my plate with my journey, and I had a day with no tears until now. Drugs are so evil; I hate them. They destroy lives. All I can do is continue to pray for him, as I do every day, and have faith that God will answer, just like I continue to have faith that Adonis will one day reply to my text.

Hi, i hope you're having a good night. I don't care about sharing anymore, I'm done with trying to be cool in front of you. I'm so comfortable to share my thoughts & feelings.

I'm fascinated with everything, it's unbelievable the more I learn the more I realise just how special we truly are .

I have this absolute fascination with the planet. The movie I chose to see today was Rachael's farm & I loved learning more about the soil how it can impact climate change. I'm absolutely so fascinated it's beautiful. I can't wait to hear one day if you are the same. It's bizarre, I mean after divorce I was making better choices cause I could chose for myself but now it's on another level, every product I buy, even face creams. Forget anti aging. For me it's about if it's organic (good for the environment, when I wash it down the sink later, not even about my skin better with organic), vegan & cruelty free (for the animals) I have such compassion. I had to give myself a talking to about not knowing any better before so now I am comfortable wearing leather shoes etc that I already have. I'm like you didn't know it's ok, just make better choices in the future. I'm just hoping my current bags, shoes last for like 20 years

Anyway that's my sharing for tonight, geezaz I can't wait to hear one day, how your journey is going, it's incredible, magic & madness all wrapped up in one

Sending so much love & light babes x

Who knows if that one day will ever come?

Love Michelle Ashton

Sunday, 6th August 2023

Dear Journal,

This weekend has been one of the best I've had in ages. Full of yummy food, a movie, a massage, and a trip to Spotlight Haberdashery. I find it really fun, like a Bunnings Hardware is for men. It's a little different from what I used to find fun on the weekend. Note to self to spend more time doing things that make you happy. Life is too short to be stressed, and it's not about material possessions. I am blessed to have a roof over my head and access to a car. Having some money is enjoyable for experiences like massages, movies, delicious meals, event tickets, and the occasional getaway or holiday. However, wonderful experiences can also be found in simple, free activities. For those lucky enough to live nearby, the beach offers the chance to breathe in the salty air and listen to the seagulls. Similarly, a park allows us to appreciate nature as a free and beautiful experience. Life is all about love, love for oneself and love for others. What a journey to go on to realise that, and how totally blessed I am.

To top off my fantastic weekend, Salma said she could come to Deepak Chopra next Friday. I was so excited, and I told her I was going makeup-free. I don't remember the last time I had the guts to go out makeup-free and feel comfortable; it's so liberating. Wow, this journey is incredible!

Love, Michelle Ashton

Monday, 7th August 2023

Dear Journal,

This morning, I realised that I have completely cut out all prescription medicine, and I'm not taking anywhere near the number of vitamins that I used to. I would joke that I rattled when I walked. I eat so healthy now and don't see why I need so many. I feel the healthiest I've ever been; I'm so happy and content. Oh my gosh, that reminds me, I have just ticked off another goal on my bed mirror. To be so happy, healthy and content, bring it on; let's get the others ticked off, too.

Love, Michelle Ashton

Tuesday, 8th August 2023

Dear Journal,

Today was fabulous, just like yesterday and the day before; now, every day is beautiful. I am loving life to a whole different degree now. I've always been one to try to see the positives, but now there is no need to try; everything honestly is fantastic. I did a Pilates class this morning at Fernwood Fitness in Rockdale. I love this women-only gym; everyone is lovely and down to earth, and the instructors are all so friendly. You can tell everyone wants to be there, from staff to members. It's such great energy. I've never been a big fan of the gym, only the results you can achieve, but I enjoy every moment in this one. They are also very patient with my challenges; that's going to be my new word for my left side; it's just a little challenging. I love the way my days start now. I need to move every day, and weights or Pilates will be enough for when Adonis finally returns. I don't think any cardio will be required, ha.

Then it was on to my absolute passion: One Kiss. When I sat down to create my Instagram content, I thought about how I had come up with the name—just another Divinely orchestrated moment. I had been racking my brain for days and days, trying to think of something I loved that was wedding-related and catchy. I was getting to the end of my rope and sitting in a Clovelly nail salon when I asked the Angels for a sign. Then, over the radio, I heard the song One Kiss. I got chills, that's it, I love it. Now, to think of the words, something in you lit up Heaven in me, seriously! I couldn't have more love for my beautiful business. I have endured so much to help all these beautiful brides that will come my way. I honestly think when people see how I live with no lounge room, they feel sorry for me. I'm so happy. Don't get me wrong, I look forward to the day when I have an office and a couch to stretch out on, but I absolutely love what I do; my passion for helping is the driver. I have seen how much brides get charged extra, and because it's such a special day for them, they go over budget; it's out of love that they do that. It doesn't have to be that way. If I won the lotto tomorrow, nothing would change. I love this business like nothing else, except for Adonis, who is my first and forever love; then, I want to help everyone else in love.

I felt so lovey-dovey that I sent this text.

Hi beautiful,

I just don't care about trying to act cool & not bat shit crazy! I am bat shit crazy for you. I just want to tell you over & over I think of you all the time & I really hope you're doing well. Sending so much love x

It feels so beautiful to be this much in love, and this is just energy. He hasn't even spoken to me. Oh my gosh, when he does, I will be the happiest girl in the world; my vibration will touch the sky. I swear that's all I need in life. I would give up everything to be in his arms forever.

Love, Michelle Ashton

Wednesday, 9th August 2023

Dear Journal,

What a day! I woke up at 6.30 am with no alarm clock; I felt so free. I naturally wake up now; I have a body clock. I will still set an alarm for early morning meetings or appointments for peace of mind; otherwise, I probably won't sleep. I will also put one on the first night I spend with Adonis, as I will be so content I will sleep forever. Just thinking about that, I may have said this before, but I cannot even imagine how happy I will feel to open my eyes first thing in the morning and see his perfect face. My life will be complete; that's all I need right there. Wow, the emotions I feel when I write that. I need to take a breather; it is so overwhelming in the best way possible.

I decided to skip the gym this morning. I do whatever I want now, and I wasn't feeling it. With my new-found attitude, I may need to look into new jeans soon. The amount that goes in compared to the energy expelled is a massive difference. Dinner last night was a yummy lentil soup with a gluten-free bread roll, a whole block of Pana Organic mint chocolate, and two gluten-free beers. This morning, after waking, I headed to the Brighton Kiosk for the yummy granola and fruit bowl, minus the cow milk yogurt. I wished they had coconut yoghurt, but it was yummy all the same.

Then, I sat on the sand to meditate, which was absolute Heaven. When I tick off my goal to buy a humble home by the beach, I will do that as much as possible. I can't imagine how happy I will be to be close enough to a beach to enjoy time there every day. My dad used to take us, even though he has some qualities I don't admire. I love him very much. He is cool; he's a bit of an old hippy. It must be where I get it from. I admire people who beat to their own drum. I also used to go daily when I lived on Havelock Avenue in Coogee; it was within walking distance of the beach. I can't believe I felt comfortable enough to sleep on it after night shifts; now, in my apartment on the 5th floor, I have the alarm on stay mode, and my bedroom has a digital door lock on the internal door.

Back at the beautiful beach this morning, I put my feet in the water, which is unheard of for me in winter. Then I had an incredible work day; let me rephrase, I had a great passion day. It's not work when it's your passion. Then, in the evening, I thought about my message last night to Adonis; I am not embarrassed. There are no secrets; his higher self knows everything about me. One day, I was in a crowded place and wanted to find a bathroom. I had to do something that women probably don't admit to doing when I heard, just fart. How embarrassing, geez Louise. No wonder I felt so comfortable when we hung out as mates those nights. We have often hung out; my 3D just doesn't remember. You can be in a relationship or a marriage for years and still have secrets, but sharing a Soul, there are none. I want to be there for him, and as much as I think he might need time, I also think I know what I want, so maybe he does, too. I will never know until we talk, so I covered my bases in every way. I don't want to scare him or think it's something I don't want, so here's my text tonight.

Darling. I really don't know how to approach this situation.

I now know how much you have obviously been through as Tf's normally have similar backgrounds & mine is just beyond there are no words to express the pain (that kills me by the way, more than anything on this whole journey to think about you in such pain. I would endure mine all over again if that meant changing your past)

So knowing what I know, please just let me know what you need. You need commitment from me you got it, you need be to take it slow you got it, you need me to back the f... off you got it you are so precious to me you really have no idea.

Whatever you need. I will work with you, please just trust me, you are so precious to me I would never hurt you intentionally or unintentionally. I know & love you x

I'm now going to do some more me time. It's my favourite thing to do these days. A bath, listening to rock-jazz covers, and a glass of wine—total bliss. Isn't my whole life at the moment; it just keeps getting better and better. Life truly is incredible. I love feeling this happy and free. I am so glad I've waffled on. One day, I will look back and smile at remembering who I am and how far I've come.

Love, Michelle Ashton

Thursday, 10th August 2023

Dear Journal,

It was another incredible day, but I came to significant realisations about how I live. I woke up at 5.30 to the sound of traffic. My bedroom faces Princes Highway. I love my apartment, but it isn't working for me anymore. I can probably only do another year in this pad. I never actually set my roots down here. I didn't have or meet any friends in the area, and the only thing I found close was my beautiful gym, everything else I travelled and used, what services I had before. It's been a great transition apartment. I nicknamed it the concrete jungle. Maybe I should have left the apartment more, and I would have found the beautiful little grass areas downstairs. Anyway, it's seen too many tears. I don't even know where I want to live. I would love a humble home as close to the water as possible. I want to be able to walk outside in the fresh air. Some people have these crazy huge mortgages and put themselves under so much stress. That's entirely the opposite of what I want; all you need for a house to be a home Is love, so I don't care for anything that doesn't support that dream—love, love, love. Love for myself too, so working eighteen hours a day is out. I want to enjoy life and have time to give all the love I have inside me to the people dear to me.

That brings me to my second major life decision made today: I need to put myself first. I am in so much pain while sitting now. I don't know if I've done something to myself from all the long periods I've spent working at my desk, driving for my NDIS work, and also for Uber. Maybe the Universe is trying to get me to get outside more because I spend too much time indoors with the blinds closed; this is so the sun doesn't damage the fabrics. I honestly don't know the answer; I finally realise that One Kiss cannot take priority over looking after myself. I almost couldn't breathe with this realisation. I felt like I wanted to throw up; I was physically nauseous. I have spent many years wanting to help all my beautiful brides and not looking after myself properly. Not eating well, just grabbing whatever I can, even if it's a bag of crisps and a coffee. Not sleeping enough, and just working myself into the ground. Luckily, I only realised this now. Otherwise, I wouldn't be where I am today. If helping through One Kiss is my destiny, the Universe will create a situation. It's as simple as that. Talk about handing the outcome over. Wow, my amount of faith in the Universe is on another level. I know it's always working for my highest good. I love sending him updates; even though I'm blocked, it feels nice. I just sent this.

I just can't thank you enough.
I've had the whole day off
Pilates
Cuppa at Brighton, love it down there In the Sun
Yummiest nourish bowl for lunch
Reike
Get home in arvo instead of jumping into work head downstairs to sit in the sun for half, then come up & before emails smash a packet of organic pea chips & a beer... seriously how

f...ing good is life, you will never know my gratitude, I remember what it's like to live, sending love, really hope your doing well

There are so many changes for the better all the time. I can't imagine who I will be in five years. I'm blessed and excited about my future. I have no idea what it all looks like, but I know it will be incredible.

Love, Michelle Ashton

Friday, 11th August 2023

Dear Journal,

I had a great time with Salma at Deepak Chopra; that man is so insightful. It really was an experience of a lifetime. How blessed we are that he shares his profound wisdom with us all. There aren't many people who get me just to shut the fork up and listen; he had me engrossed for hours. To top it off, I also got to spend time with Salma. We get each other like no other; she knows about Adonis and my love for him. We were chatting about men on the way, and she didn't understand why I didn't even look at others.

The conversation went a little like, you don't get it; I only have eyes for him. No one else catches my attention. I have blinkers on, and I certainly don't give off that signal for anyone to approach me. Salma asks what would happen if someone was all sexy and just grabbed you. My immediate reaction would be to punch them in the face. How forking ridiculous. I am so in love with someone who couldn't give two shits about me. How long am I expected to wait?

I love my life now and don't want to waste it. I want to experience real love; it's about bloody time. I don't know how to give anyone a chance, but I won't find out if I don't put myself out there. I'm going to bed alone again, just like I've done for over ten years. Ian and I had separate bedrooms. He moved out of our shared room not long after my brain surgery. I was 36 years old. I was alone whilst married, and I'm still alone and sick of it; I want to experience life.

Love, Michelle Ashton

Saturday, 12th August 2023

Dear Journal,

This text sums up my feelings this morning.

Good morning beautiful,

Happy Saturday!

I know how you hate texts, here's a f... ing book of my feelings.

I have woken up sad & determined to live my life.

You have given me more than you will ever know. You saved my life, I allowed others to treat me bad, I treated myself bad, never putting my needs first. No wonder I took drugs, why wouldn't I be looking to escape my shitty life, no more, ever! I love my life & I like to treat myself so well. I do know something is still missing, intimacy! I didn't have sex with anyone before you, after my ex & I haven't been with anyone after. I've been single for years now & I had sex once on the 4th of Jan 2023. It's just sad.

Salma knows the situation & asked me if I look at others & I said, I simply have eyes for no other, absolutely no one, complete blinkers on. I don't give off that vibe whatsoever for anyone to approach me & she said what happens if they were all sexy & just grabbed you & I said my first reaction would be to punch them in the face! I can't keep allowing myself to be like that. I have come so far with this healing.

I have done everything in my power to energetically pave the way for you, you have no idea what has been going on behind the scenes. So much healing & it has been so tough (what an understatement) I have completely got rid of everything from my ex, nothing remains, except my hyphenated surname which I only ever use for my licence, my bank etc. I am so free, I have sold, given to charity, even thrown in the forking bin, expensive stuff. One friend said are you serious when I told them one thing I threw down the garbage shoot but it just felt so f...ing good, along with blocking him out of my life. I even blocked your ex too, even though why would she ever call me but I said to Salma, I imagine it would be like Adonis being friends with my ex, that would be f...ing weird so I just decided to block & I would do that with anyone else that would ever have a problem. No one will ever stand in the way of my happiness!

I have been so vulnerable with you for months & months now do you think it's been easy to continue to put myself out there & never get anything in return. I have completely put aside my pride. Made myself look totally insane. I put everything on the line for just the slightest chance you would even entertain a conversation with me. I have just gone after what I want with everything I have. healing, energetically, tried to put into words, even though these texts don't even scratch the surface.

All this vulnerability & not one ounce of vulnerability in return, can you imagine if the shoe was on the other foot babe, try to see things from my point of view.

You are everything to me & I am nothing to you!
I hope you realise, that I am important to you & you're important to you, before it's too late. I really do but there is simply nothing I can do about it anymore, I wave the white flag babe.

I love you so much & always will. You will always my perfect Adonis.

Now, to get on with my day. I finally dragged myself out of bed and scrubbed off my number one goal. I also did that a little while back but wrote it again: this journey does that to you. I've been used by men in the past, but this certainly is a new one for Spiritual ascension; that's a first. I know myself well enough to know when I'm done, I'm done, so I hope he doesn't wait too long. I don't know what my time frame for feelings looks like. I will always love that beautiful man who saved my life, but in terms of a relationship, when I do eventually move on. I would never hurt someone who did nothing to me, not in my wildest dreams.

My man will never have to question my love or if they are living in someone else's shadow; when I love someone, I love hard. Adonis had better put his skates on; my patience is wearing thin. I'm doing something I never thought I could do. I'm not blocking. If he wants to call me, he can, and hopefully, it's not too late. I am deleting his contact information. I don't know his number by heart and will not look.

Here is my last text before I delete

My heart is racing like it never has, I am showing strength & to myself that I never knew I had. Wow, I feel like I'm going to throw up but I just have to do it & im not peaking at your number before & I don't know it off by heart so here goes. I'm not blocking you babe, you are so more than welcome to call me anytime. I just won't know it's you as I'm deleting your contact. I simply have to stop myself from texting you. I can hardly breathe when I write this but I know I have to.

Ball really is in your court my beautiful Adonis, sending love & once I press this button, I will have to pick myself up off the floor, my throat is tightening. Omfg sending so much love & I really do hope you call or we cross paths in the future x

I can't breathe; the tears are like nothing I've ever experienced, and my throat is so tight. What the fork have I done? I know I needed to, but arrrrrrrrrrrrrrrrrrrr. I did it; I deleted his contact. I pick up my phone. The name is gone, but some texts remain with just the number on top, which I can see clearly. The Universe works in the most mysterious ways. Did I pass the test?

Whilst I'm in a world of pain, I act like I'm fine when Seb calls. He has enough on his plate; I don't want to add to it. He shares his good news: he's off for a holiday in Port Douglas. I love that place; I'm obsessed with a church right by the water, so infatuated that I have it in with my will documents for my bro. That's where I want my ashes spread; Im not sure about the legalities; he will have to work that out, I won't be here to help. I honestly wonder what my absolute fascination with that church is; it is the most beautiful little church I have ever seen; it takes my breath away.

It's now so late in the afternoon. I've had a very slow start. I still have lots of shopping to do. I got in the car to go to Westfield Bondi Junction and thought I should go to a local shopping mall, but It was late, and I knew where all the stores were. Then I heard, you have to learn sometime. I love how guided I am, though I didn't take the advice; I'm in a rush today. I had frequented the same mall since it opened in 2004, when I worked for Westpac Bank, right before my infamous receptionist gig at Misty's massage parlour. I know this mall like the back of my hand. I need to find a new one, but I must first work out where I want to live. Until recently, I had lived in the eastern suburbs of Sydney since I was sixteen. My life isn't there anymore, and I don't want it to be. It was lovely, but it's not me. I now recognise that. My bogan bohemian lifestyle isn't a match for the East, and that is fine; each to their own. Let's go where our heart sings. I don't know where that is for me, but I know it isn't in the East.

Later in the evening, Salma called in the absolute best mood, she has such a passion for soccer and Australia had won. I love hearing her so happy, but even more so that I was the one she wanted to share the news with. I love that girl so much; she is such a special Soul. It's been such a long emotional day, I'm off to bed before midnight. I'm such a rager these days.

Love, Michelle Ashton

Sunday, 13th August 2023

Dear Journal,

This morning, I added new goals to my bedroom mirror.
12. Learn to ride a bike again.
13. Work on left arm and balance.
14. Learn to swim with my challenging left arm.
15. Learn to paddle board
(great for balance, but better learn to swim first, ha)

I'm trying to stay positive, and it's tough when you are in so much pain. I can hardly sit still. This is so embarrassing; not only do I have a sore butt, my female bits are killing me. I went to the doctor for tests, thinking maybe I had caught something from Adonis. Everything came back clear. Doc said it could be a menopause symptom, but I went through menopause prematurely; it was years back. I can't remember the last time I had a period. I am given some cream; why have I never heard of this problem? Are women embarrassed to talk about it? I've heard of hot flushes but not vaginal dryness. It's not working; I'm still in pain. I was guided to a gynaecologist at the Women's Health and Research Institute of Australia, but I don't have private health insurance. The monthly premiums were too expensive, so I had to cancel. Unfortunately, Medicare doesn't cover all of the costs. I have to find the money and book an appointment; the pain is forking excruciating.

Love, Michelle Ashton

Mon 14th August 2023

Dear Journal,

I'm so not in the mood for anything. I just put some comfy trackies on, I'm in absolute agony. WTF is going on? I can't even journal anymore today.

Love, Michelle Ashton

Tuesday, 15th August 2023

Dear Journal,

I'm in so much pain I can't go to the gym this week. I am really worried, and I want to be able to make love to Adonis when he returns. Right now, I can't even sit down comfortably. I've given my body to others, I've had sex, but I have never made love. I wonder what it feels like. I imagine feeling that close to someone would be the most beautiful experience. I don't ever want to go back to only having sex with a partner. I want to make love to them, but first, I need to work out what is wrong with me, and that's not the only issue; I also have a raging sore throat. I have had it for years, but it's at its worst. I was guided to a holistic doctor in Surry Hills, and my appointment is later today.

First up is my passion, One Kiss. I wish I had a standing desk. It's only just launched, and the margins are so tiny that I can't even think about the extra expense. I want to be a disruptor in this lucrative industry. I would have loved to set it up officially as a not-for-profit, but it's so challenging that I just keep the margins almost non-existent. I don't need much, maybe just an office and a couch. My desire to help others is so deep that I need to find a way to do that without working myself into the ground.

It's doc appointment time, and I'm seeing Nick Bassal, who founded the Wholistic Medical Centre in 1977. Over the years, I've seen countless doctors and had many tests and treatments. Not one fixed the problem; it always returned. I even resorted to having my tonsils removed trying to solve the mystery; it's quite a painful operation at forty years old. This doctor is the only one who asked me emotional questions regarding my physical symptoms that resonated. No wonder I was guided to him; what an intuitive doctor. I have been dealing with this issue for years. He gets some background information and asks about home life; we chat about my marriage and divorce. He asks if I find it hard to swallow when I get stressed. Yes, I do. Doctor Nick explains that's where the term "I'm choked up comes from" and to think back to when it started; what was happening in my life? Energy can be caught up in the throat chakra when we don't have a voice or aren't speaking our minds.

Have I suffered all these years because I didn't tell Ian what a piece of shit husband he was? He knows how he treated me; God does, too; he sees everything. I'm going home to get the picture album I made of the two of us and burn the forking thing. Actually, why should the environment suffer because he is an arsehole? I will enjoy every moment of ripping it into a million pieces; I never want to see his face again! I will never let anyone who doesn't have my best interests at heart anywhere near me. I am going to treat myself how I should have all along. I will not be taken advantage of ever again. I will be bloody choosy when deciding who will be in my space. I have such high standards now. Come proper, Adonis, or as much as it will kill me, don't come at all.

What a forking day! I'm not coping well; I'm so spent, but I have an 8 pm Akashic records session that I am excited about. I love healing now. I can't imagine being on my deathbed and never knowing what it was like to truly live. Bring on the healing baby!

Love, Michelle Ashton

Wednesday, 16th August 2023

Dear Journal,

After the Akashic records session last night, I woke up in the middle of the night crying my eyes out. I don't know if it was a nightmare or if I'm being guided to deal with something. It goes back to when I lived in Bondi Beach at number 178 Campbell Parade for three years, from 2011 to 2014. It was so long ago, but something awful may have happened to me.

I remember not long after my brain surgery, waking up at my front door with the key in the door and my beloved fur baby hiding around the corner; he seemed so scared. I must have been really hammered not to remember how I got there. I was drinking quite heavily in those days, at least a couple of bottles of wine a night, just another way of escaping. I still drink now, but only a couple, not like that; I have nothing to escape from. I had a hubby who wasn't the man I needed; I had just had brain surgery. I knew I was lucky to be alive, but I was angry; I was angry at all the doctors I had seen previously complaining of these insane headaches. All these new challenges I faced could have been avoided if any of those doctors had found the tumour earlier. I had a victim mentality and was alone most of the time whilst my ex was in Bali every month. He used to take me with him until he started having an affair with one of his staff. Ian vehemently denied this, but others in Bali told me. It was a juicy rumour; my woman's intuition knew it was true, yet I chose to believe my husband, and quite frankly, I had enough going on in my life.

Ian was away on this occasion, probably hooking up with rumour chick. I asked my friend Lilith, who lived directly below us in apartment 20, what time I had left her place. I was trying to put the pieces together. She laughed when I told her I had woken up on my doorstep. I have a feeling something terrible happened; I wish I could remember. Did someone on my apartment floor know what happened? Where I lived and that I had an alarm that would have gone off if the front door had been opened? I changed everything around so I could take a hypnotherapy appointment I was guided to; it's tomorrow, only one more day. I need to try to get to the bottom of this. I feel sick, I'm so scared, I cry so much just writing this. It's lunchtime, and I'm still in my pj's at the computer. I wish I could crawl into bed, fork life is so tough sometimes. When does it get easier? God, when, please tell me. I know it's for my highest good, but I'm in so much pain right now; what's tomorrow afternoon going to be like?

Love, Michelle Ashton

Thursday, 17th August 2023

Dear Journal,

I'm going to get out of my pyjamas this morning. I stayed in them all day yesterday until it was time to shower and meet Salma. It was just one of those days. This journal has become such an outlet for my thoughts and feelings. Since I share everything, I have been googling some of my female physical symptoms down there. I can't wait to be able to afford to see the gyno and find out if this is correct: It all seems to match. Sensitive nerves, on the surface, can be caused by lack of sex, well check. Things that can make it worse are menopause, sitting for long periods, stress, wearing tight clothing, not eating well or taking care of yourself, check check check check check check. When I get this fixed, and make love to my Adonis. I will be a brand-new girl, just like Madonna's song, Like a Virgin, touched for the very first time.

Then I was heading into Surry Hills for my dreaded hypnotherapy appointment; walking to the train station, my foot was sore too; it still gives me grief years later. In 2016, whilst living with Ian in Rose Bay, I fell down a few stairs and broke my heel bone. I'm a bloody mess; luckily, I got out of that marriage alive. It's a rare fracture, accounting for only about 2% of all adult fractures. It's unbelievable that I broke it; falling down a couple of stairs, a car crash, a fall from a ladder, or another high-energy event is usually the cause. I told Ian I thought I had broken my foot, as it was so bloody sore. He was drunk and high, the same as I was, and told me not to be ridiculous and just go to bed. I did what I was told and woke to a foot the size of an elephant in the morning. Ian couldn't carry me, so I had to get down the stairs to his car; the pain, fork me!

In the emergency department at St Vincent's Public Hospital, it was confirmed that I had a fracture and that it was my calcaneus bone. The unfortunate thing for me was because of my balance issues, I couldn't use crutches. I had a walking frame and a wheelchair. We had stairs in Rose Bay, so when Ian was at work, I was confined to my bedroom upstairs; it had a bathroom, but the kitchen was downstairs. I had a couple of up & go protein shakes to get me through the day, but I was always so hungry when Ian came home. During this time, he also went on a so-called business trip to Vegas with his son. I checked into a hotel, so at least I could eat via room service. Ian was working so hard that he was completely smashed out of his mind whenever we spoke.

That reminds me of another time he left me to get wasted with his son when I needed him. I was in hospital and had just suffered an anaphylactic attack. I went through a stage when I had so many allergies. I was left alone in St Vincents Public so he could go out for a celebrity lunch at Luke Mangan's restaurant in the Sydney Hilton Hotel. I drove myself home from the hospital, and hours later, he returned belligerent and drunk as a skunk.

Luke Mangan and his wife were friends of ours. I met the lovely couple in Bali in 2010, before my brain surgery and his wife's breast cancer; she's a courageous survivor. The four of us had a lot of fun together; we all enjoyed food, wine, and laughter and would catch up for dinners in Oz and overseas. I had even cooked for the couple in our Tamarama home; that must have been a real treat for the Australian chef and restaurateur Luke Mangan. My heart was in the right place. I thought cooking for someone of his calibre was intimidating, so he probably doesn't get a home-cooked meal a lot. I had been taking cooking classes with the talented Maria Benardis from Greekalicious and thought I would take on the challenge. I didn't kill him with my kindness, and we remained friends until Ian and my seperation in 2021, though after tasting my culinary delights, we always went out for meals, and he cooked for us at his home. At one point, Ian and I lived in the same suburb, an affluent harbourside area in the eastern suburbs of Sydney.

Ian had met Luke through his mate Richard Branson. Luke was the chef for Virgin Airlines. Ian had previously served as the CEO of the Virgin Entertainment Group, where he opened more than 20 Virgin Megastores, including the world-famous store in Times Square, New York. I have met Richard Branson, he is so lovely. The first time was on New Year's Eve in 2006 when he and his wife, Joan, hosted a party on a catamaran in Sydney Harbour. Over the years, we have socialised a couple more times. Ian and I were invited to the Virgin Australia Launch Party, which was held on Sydney's Cockatoo Island. Our friends Lilith and Andrew, who also worked for the company, attended. Another time, we were asked to a small gathering for lunch at Icebergs Dining Room in Bondi, which pals of ours tagged along, including my old friend Peter. We have also shared drinks at a Darlinghurst bar, but he was Ian's friend. Ian and his son would catch up with Richard whenever he was in town. Ian and Richard's sons are close. Once, Richard's son Sam was accidentally peed on by my puppy Pucci, who was only a few months old at the time; how embarrassing, ha!

Back to today, I reached Central Station, and after the short walk, I arrived at the office of Doctor Tracie O'Keefe. I'm so scared that I might uncover something that will make being intimate even harder. I already have so many issues. I look around and realise I am always guided in the right direction. This hypnotherapist has degrees all over the wall. She is the most highly qualified and experienced clinical hypnotherapist, psychotherapist, counsellor, and mental health professional practising in Australia today, and is also a number one best-selling Amazon author. I have previously had hypnotherapy to give up smoking, but something tells me this session is going to be a lot harder. My mind is put at ease when Doctor O'Keefe is kind, caring, and patient. I am taken back to that night; I can't work out if I was drugged. I explained to her that I drank heavily and took a lot of drugs at the time, so feeling crap the next day wasn't out of the ordinary. I could not see anything, but the tears were uncontrollable. Doc stated that it was apparent something so traumatic happened that night, and my unconscious mind wouldn't let me see right now. It only shows you what you are ready to deal with, and that's ok. We will just put the traumatic event in a box and place it in the back of the mind. I leave the appointment feeling a little lighter, but wondering if my box will stay shut.

I told Salma that I couldn't recall the traumatic event and also divulged to her that I had worked in a massage parlour; I was so ashamed to say that to her as it's not the person I am. She assures me she knows that and loves me. You would think that's the place where something traumatic might happen, or the nightclubs with drug fiends and dealers, not your bloody apartment building. I was hell-bent on how forked drugs were before. Suppose I wouldn't have been so smashed all the time; I may have been able to understand that I felt so crap that day after, and it was not just another day until the night when you start all over again. Drugs are so evil, and you think it's harmless; you're just having a good time, and if your friends do it well, it's normal, right? Anyone who uses drugs is escaping from something, even if it's something they are not aware of. In the eastern suburbs of Sydney, A-class drugs are prevalent, especially cocaine. You think it's cooler because it costs more. How stupid! At 3 - $500 a gram, you're just paying more money to escape. If you truly love your life, why would you want to escape, and hurt yourself? It's not fun to hurt yourself.

I am so grateful for Adonis coming into my life, but I think I've put it all to bed now. I love him so much, and our 5D's will always be connected, but in the 3D, he is better off without me. I'm way too messed up; he shouldn't have to deal with my childhood, teenage, and all the trauma from my adult years, plus all my physical challenges; there is no throwing me on a surfboard. I have no qualifications or degrees. I'm completely daft at times. I can't cook. I'm not rich, and I'm a total bogan. The list could go on and on. He is better off learning to deal with my energy and finding a sweet, pristine girl who treats him well. I love him so much, I want the absolute best for him, and that's not me.

I just added a new goal to mirror that says

New goal surpasses all others.
I want peace above everything, please, Universe.
If I could only get one wish, it would be peace!

Love, Michelle Ashton

Friday, 18th August 2023

Dear Journal,

I thought yesterday was tough. I woke up at 4:30 a.m., distressed like I've never been. I said, leave me alone; please, you're hurting me. I thought we were friends. Oh my forking gosh, I know the person. I feel so sick. I hear she's waking up; get her out of here, no more. I cry uncontrollably and sit on my kitchen floor; I get paper and start writing everything down to piece it together. I had only just recovered from brain surgery and learned to walk again. A stranger wouldn't have known this, but a friend would have been aware of all I had just been through and that I was lucky to be alive. Who, who could do this? Seriously, what kind of person?

I remember another incident that I had previously blocked out. My ex-husband was meant to go to Bali, as he usually did every month. This was only a month after I had woken up at my door; he decided not to go on that trip. I used to sit out on the balcony, getting completely smashed and smoking my head off. Ian was in his bedroom asleep. I had left our Bondi apartment with no shoes, no key, nothing, and I was running up Campbell Parade; that was a shock in itself, let alone the fact that I had shit myself. I am banging on Hotel Ravesis's door; they have just closed and are cleaning up. They won't let me in; I don't blame them; I have no shoes, I smell like booze, shit, and I'm jittery. Had I seen the person who assaulted me? If I hadn't bolted, would it have happened again? Have I seen them since? Who are they? Forking hell. How did they know Ian was supposed to be away? Are they a friend of his? I think, why wouldn't I run to my husband? I hear he didn't protect you; he should have been there to protect you.

I return to our Bondi penthouse, and buzzing the doorbell wakes Ian up. He lets me in and asks why I was outside. I say "I don't know, I don't know." Why was this not bizarre? Your wife is in that state with no shoes, no key, smells like crap and has no idea why? I thought he really didn't give a shit; he had checked out of our marriage. Just like he did with his ex-wife previous to me, his family lived in Montecito, whilst Ian lived at the Four Seasons Hotel in Beverly Hills during the week. He would drive home for the weekends, leaving his mistress in L.A. This went on for six long years, and I'm questioning why he didn't care that I was outside with shit in my pants in the middle of the night. I also remember having PTSD; I would jump at the slightest thing. I figured it was the aftermath of the brain surgery. I remember this now because I'm jumpy again; it's making sense. No wonder I felt so comfortable at a women's gym. What kind of man could hurt a woman? That's not a man. That's a pathetic piece of shit. I'm jumping around just like my mind, nerves, and heart beat right now.

Back to 4:30 a.m., when I was sitting on my kitchen floor, I smelled smoke. That's weird; the smoke alarm wasn't going off. I checked my apartment, but nothing. Then I heard, something's burning, get out. I don't know where this all fits in. I don't know if someone called me the night I ran out of the house, whether I heard it outside on the balcony or on the TV. I don't know. What are my guides trying to tell me? I'm scared to go to sleep; what more would I discover? It's so forking hard; no wonder people stay in the dark for their whole lives; this is petrifying. I know I need to work it out and get to the bottom of it, but I'm fearful. I've never been this frightened in my entire life; what will I see? Who will I know? I pray that whatever it is, I don't see my beloved fur baby having to witness it; that would have terrified him. Will I ever find out the answers? Whoever you are, God knows he sees everything, and the Universe has my back!

Michelle Ashton

Saturday, 19th August 2023

Dear Journal,

I slept for a few hours last night but feel even sicker today. I'm starting to piece things together, and the amount of trust I had and continued to have for over a decade after is incomprehensible. It concerns two robberies. The first was a break-in at Vaucluse, an incredibly affluent area of the eastern suburbs known for its peninsular and harbour views; our home had a birdseye view of the Sydney Harbour Bridge and Opera House. The second fictitious robbery was at Tamarama, a small and exclusive beachside suburb in the eastern suburbs. This property was located in the area's most sought-after and tightly held cul de sac, with unobstructed beach and ocean views. The first break-in at Vaucluse was so scary that afterwards, we never felt comfortable. For me, this triggered a childhood wound. In hindsight, I probably didn't need to be that scared; this was when we sold our home and moved to Tamarama, which has a very low property crime rate in Sydney. This horrific crime happened to me because of a lie. I lied for my ex-husband. Anyone close to me knows I'm the most honest person. I lied and continued to keep the secret for years because it was so severe that it could send my husband to jail for insurance fraud. My loyalty came before my honesty.

The first was an actual break-in at our home in Vaucluse; many things were stolen, including the entire safe. We returned from Bali one day early, and that night, we went to The Comedy Store in Moore Park. We were laughing our heads off and couldn't hear the alarm company, ADT, calling us. Once outside, we got the news and headed straight home. Walking into our property took me back to when I was a child. It is so scary; you are unsure if anyone is still on the property; we heard noises upstairs, so we ran out and immediately called the police. They were incredible and took it very seriously. Moments later, multiple cars arrive, and a police helicopter is hovering over our home. The sirens were so loud, and I couldn't tell how many armed officers had entered the property. They hear the noises and are at the bottom of the stairs, shouting, "This is the police; we have you surrounded; come out with your hands up." The noises continue. These thieves are undeterred, and the police head up the stairs with their guns ready to fire. This is surreal. They found the culprit hiding under the bed; he looked so scared as he was led down the stairs. He runs to me, and I hold him so tight. Even though he isn't allowed upstairs, he is forgiven this time. My poor fur baby, Cisco, is terrified; he wasn't bred to be a watchdog.

My late grandfather was in the police force for 30 years. I know he watches over me and wouldn't be proud of the moment that I lied and continued to. I speak to him in my prayers; I say "I'm going to dream until my dreams come true." Every day, I say the same thing. It may take me a little while to get my head back together, but when I do, my dreams will become a reality. Pop, I love you so much, and I'm sorry I lied.

After the police had been through, we looked around, and most of the cupboards and closets were trashed, except my dressing room; it was pretty neat compared to the rest of the home. As you would find in a store, these big jewellery displays housed all my costume jewellery. They sat on a centre console, still upright in the same spot, and several pieces remained; it looked like other items had been carefully removed. WTF, why would the thieves care about my things in particular? I found my engagement and wedding ring in the bowl that I kept them in; it was at the back of my closet; they must have missed this. I let Ian know, and he told me to be quiet and informed the police that these pieces were also in the stolen safe. Afterwards, I said you can't say that; it's forking wrong; it's illegal. Ian explained that Insurance premiums are expensive enough, so it's only fair, and everyone adds extra items to their stolen lists. I know it's wrong, but he pays the bills, so I comply with my husband.

After we move into Tamarama, we are partying one night, and a few friends are with us. My new larger engagement ring, which Ian had bought me with proceeds from the insurance claim, is missing. How did we get robbed while sitting around getting high? Did someone sneak in, and we didn't notice? Fork, we must have been so smashed. I'm devastated that this could happen again. I want to call the police; Ian doesn't want to because we just had a claim and explains it will look fishy. I don't want my husband to get into trouble, so I agree, but I'm sad that I have no ring. Ian announces that he wants to make me happy and will buy another but blames Peter as there was no forced entry, and he was there that night. Ian discussed that he is bad news and wants him out of our lives. I can't believe this could be true. I agree he is dangerous, but not with me; I have known him for years, but even so, I took my husband's side and cut

Peter out of my life, and most of my friends did, too. We all think he is a thief.

A while later, I found my engagement ring in a jacket pocket; WTF, I'm in disbelief. I always put my ring in the same bowl, but it wasn't there. Why would I put it in a jacket pocket? I have never done that before. It's a very expensive item that could have ended up at the bloody drycleaners. I told Ian, and he said you forking idiot, you were so smashed you forgot, and now everyone thinks Peter is a thief. I have never felt so guilty and ashamed. I'm such an honest person, and this is eating me up, but I can't admit the truth, as we can't have anyone questioning the first robbery and, therefore, Ian's fraudulent Insurance claim. I cannot risk my husband going to jail to clear my conscience and Peter's name, so I continue to lie.

This is not the only time I have lied for my ex-husband when the police have been involved. Whilst we lived in Rose Bay, Ian was a director of IOT Group, a publicly listed company on the Australian Stock Exchange. The Australian Federal Police arrived in the wee hours of the morning with a warrant to search our home. They are probably the only ones who saw with their own eyes our separate unmade beds, as we don't usually have guests that early in the morning unless they had been there partying the night before, and therefore, no one was sleeping. We are in our pyjamas, watched over by officers, whilst our home is being searched from one room to the next. They take Ian's papers and laptop as he phones his lawyer, who arrives shortly after. I tell the police I know nothing. I don't tell them I thought it sounded like a Ponzi scheme. I wouldn't put my husband in the firing line, and anyway, I had no proof; whenever I asked questions, the backlash was not worth it. I learned early on not to confront him and to mind my own business, though I did tell my brother and a good friend that they should take their money out. I didn't tell them why, and they both disregarded my opinion and, like many others, believed my fraudster husband and lost money.

Back to the night when I got my Karma for lying. It was late, and I was drunk; Ian was away, and I phoned my friend Lilith to see if she was still up and wanted to have a drink. I was looking to get high. Lilith always had coke; she would get it from Peter. What I'm piecing together so far is that I don't think she knew what would happen to me. She answers and replies yes, she can have one drink, and then she is going to bed. Sweet, I've heard this before, a couple of lines later, and it's never one drink. I walk down the fire stairs we used to get to each other's floors, taking my fur baby Pucci. Once Inside, the lights are down, and no music is playing like she usually has. Why is this being shown to me? I don't understand. I wake up from my sleep here in 2023 crying and saying, "Please, please, please, please stop" "You're hurting me so bad, please stop" "We're supposed to be friends; why are you doing this?" I get asked about this lie, and I keep repeating how sorry I am, and I hear you lying c*nt; tell me you like it. Next, I feel like I'm kind of passing out; you know that feeling when you're in hospital, about to go under general anaesthetic? Just before I do, I say, "I'm sorry; Ian made me, Ian made me." I wonder what happened to me once I was unconscious. They also know I'm not with my ex-husband anymore and have a little insight into the relationship; it makes me feel so sick that these people were involved. Oh my forking gosh, no wonder I blocked this out. I knew the three perpetrators well.

Peter Laforest, whom I met when I was sixteen years old, was the client who first coaxed me into massage. We had dated and, until not long before this night, had been extremely close friends for years and years. He was like a second husband to me; we were that close. I cannot believe that he would do this. I knew he was a drug dealer and had business in prostitution, and there were rumours of slavery and pedophilia, but this was me; we loved each other. Soon after this night, the other two perpetrators informed me that my old friend Peter had gone to jail, and they were pissed off with him because, as a result, the police had raided Lilith's chain of massage parlours.

Andrew Denman, I had known for years, too; I met him through his partner, another perpetrator of this crime; they had been dating long before Ian and me. I had known him for a considerable length of time. My shock about Peter's involvement is one thing. Andrew, I thought, was a stand-up guy; I didn't know of any skeletons in his closet. I need to question my judgment big time. There were clues that I hadn't picked up until now. Like a dinner the four of us had shared at a Mexican restaurant in Bondi. He commented on my underwear; I remember looking at him strangely, especially when his partner commented that I had lost so much weight. I explained to her that I had just done a lingerie photo shoot for my husband's 10th wedding anniversary present, and even though it was a woman photographer, I felt so uncomfortable; it was bloody nerve-racking. What I didn't say was that I had stepped so far out of my comfort zone in the hope of still being able to turn my husband on. I never stopped trying, and you knew first-hand how hard it would be. I just chalked the underwear comment up to a coincidence: Andrew Denman, you make me forking sick.

This perpetrator being involved is the hardest pill to swallow. I'm not sure I will ever be able to digest this one. Lilith Denman and I were so close that we had very few secrets. Scarcely anyone knew of my past, and she didn't judge or divulge; our friendship was like a breath of fresh air. Lilith knew me before my husband, after and everything in between. Our friends and family members mingled; there was never a special event that we didn't share. We had been through thick and thin together, including the aftermath of the rape she endured from someone close. Lilith was horrified that her perpetrator had shared breakfast with her when she had no recollection of the rape. The empathy I had for her. One breakfast, how about over a decade of meals, drinks, chats, laughs, events, memorable moments, and unconditional love? Fork me, one breakfast sounds like a taste of the Karma she deserves. Forking disgrace of a human. She is in the pictures of almost every special moment of my adult life, including the mental ones. How will I ever be able to forget her and what she did to me? I can't erase my whole life. It's unfathomable that someone could be so evil.

How will I ever trust anyone again? I still don't know if my beautiful fur baby Pucci had to witness his mum in pain. I didn't get to have kids, so he was my baby, my absolute pride and joy. In November 2021, I had to say goodbye; Lilith and Andrew sent flowers and chocolates, saying how sorry they were. I was so distraught that I couldn't speak, so I sent them both a text message.

You guys are so beautiful, thank you so much, you are so thoughtful & Pucci loved George so much, thanks guys.

George is their dog. Are you serious? My baby is in Heaven; he was with me that night. The only positive thing is that I don't understand them one iota. If I could, I'd be worried. I don't want anyone near me. I'm shutting myself off from the world for a bit. I need time alone, and when I do come back stronger than ever; I know I will. I don't want anything to do with my old life. I honestly don't care what anyone thinks about me moving on. A couple of friendships will always have a special place in my heart. For example, my wise guy knows what he means to me. Just because you love someone doesn't mean staying in each other's lives forever; we can change our life course. I don't want to stay in that energy; I'm petrified of any of it. I think if I saw an old friend, I would run for my life. I do not want to be around anything or anyone who reminds me of my bad decisions and what happened to me. Drugs are forking evil; I want nothing to do with them or any association. I want to experience every minute of my new life, one that isn't filled with moments I can't remember.

Later, I saw Reiki Angel; we are working on balancing my nervous system. I explained that I hadn't been eating, and she reminded me how important it was. I agree and say I'll go upstairs to the cafe for lunch. I have to sit in the corner in the cold doorway. I can't have anyone behind me, especially men. Fork me, this isn't going to be easy. I manage to eat a few mouthfuls, and now I'm off to the phone shop to get a new number. I've had the same one, 0402 006 006, a gold phone number for 17 years. My new one will only go to my family and Salma, who has never touched drugs in her life. I will have to work out how to deal with One Kiss later; my priority is my life and safety right now.

I am walking out of the phone shop, and for the first time in days, I'm smiling. I've got my new number and am about to start my new life. I get into my car and think about what happened to me when I was unconscious; it makes me feel so ill. I have no idea. What did they do to me? Is there anything wrong with me that I don't know about? Is the pain in the butt associated, and the vaginal pain not about being older or no sex ex. The Twin Flame journey does bring everything to the surface that needs to be healed, but this is beyond frightening, even more so thinking about what could have happened. Should I get internal checks, ultrasounds, or X-rays? I will tell my new doctor next week. I already decided I was going off the East a little while ago; my higher self was getting me ready. I am blessed to be so connected. I don't know what's physically wrong with me, but I do know for sure: I won't have to worry about running into those guys in Heaven.

Driving back into my car park, I see that someone is behind me. I pull over to let them pass to ensure they have a swipe card; how much longer will I be scared for? I'm a grown woman, and I'm frightened. Even sitting is so painful. Is it all connected? What did they forking do to me?

What did my friend watch them do? I seriously can't reconcile it. What do I expect from a woman who sells other women to make money? The devil does have a face.

I keep saying the same thing over and over. What happened to me when I was unconscious? Then I hear you don't want to know. What the fork? How do they live with themselves, especially Lilith? How did she act like such a good friend for years? I know she has done some bad shit in her life, but how could she, to me. I wouldn't hurt a fly. I hope she's having nightmares like me; at least, I know mine will get easier with time. God won't let hers subside, buckle in bitch; I've heard it's hot downstairs!

It's after midnight; I don't want to go to sleep. I'm terrified, and I lie on the floor next to my bed, crying. I start getting flashbacks. Andrew's penis is in my mouth, and he is saying you like sucking cock, don't you? I can't imagine the amount of pain on the night; right now, I can hardly breathe. How long did I have to endure this pain? How many more voices and flashbacks am I going to have? When will I be able to sleep, function, and recover enough that I don't jump through the roof when I hear a noise? I have many questions, the most important being, will I ever feel safe?

I'm not sure I will ever trust anyone ever again. How could I? Only days ago, I walked around happy and unafraid of people. I like to play the smile game. You smile at everyone you see. I read it some years ago; it's beautiful; it makes you and someone else feel good. Now, I don't want to look anyone in the eye, let alone smile at them. I can't allow this to change the person I am. They can ruin their lives, but they will not ruin mine; fork them well and truly. I hope they will one day read my journal entries and realise everyone knows what kind of people they are. I know how much God loves me; I bet they can't say the same.

I am grabbing my neck, trying to breathe. Was I choked? These flashbacks are getting intense. I can't make sense of everything I am being shown. I now know to listen to my higher self, but I'm confused, so I journal everything to put the pieces together. Not being able to breathe doesn't stop. Weren't they worried they would have a dead body in their apartment? I've never heard squeals like this, and my butt hole is hurting so much, I haven't even had anal sex with a partner. My vagina is burning with pain. I don't understand how any person, let alone a woman, could bear to hear someone in such agony. Did my baby Pucci have to listen to his mummy like this? That thought is more unbearable than anything. You absolute forking see you next Tuesday's.

No wonder I have had butt issues for years. Is it not allergies or gluten intolerance? It started precisely around that time. I thought it was from the brain surgery. I have had immune and allergy issues for years now. Trauma can cause food allergies. This phenomenon, dictated by lifestyle, stress, or trauma, can weaken the immune system and increase allergic or allergy-like reactions. I had just survived brain surgery, fighting for my life only months before. Evil doesn't even begin to scratch the surface.

The squeals continue; I want to throw up; did I throw up on the night? I keep grabbing my front bits; the pain is unbearable. The squealing is like a choking, can't-breathe noise I have never heard before tonight. It's agony to hear, and it's not even happening right now; no wonder I blocked it out all these years. One squeal goes on for so long until I pass out from the pain. Then I hear Lilith say, guys, that's enough. Did you finally get a conscious bitch?

It's now after one am I'm not tired, but im completely exhausted; I have no energy whatsoever. My front bits are burning in pain. I can't work out why; I just keep holding them, and then I hear you, dirty c*nt. They are putting something on the front whilst shoving another object in my butt hole. The squeals are terrifying; what are they putting in my anus. I'm holding my front and saying, stop, stop. The squeals are so loud I'm worried the cops will be called to my apartment now, in 2023. I wonder why no one called the police that night; then I remember the building was almost empty in 2012. The four of us had moved into our apartments before settlement. There was a legal issue, so we rented from the developers before they obtained the certification needed.

The begging and pleading continue: please stop, please stop, please. I'm going to die; I'm going to die! I'm going to die. You're going to kill me; you're going to kill me; please stop, please, I'm begging you. I'm going to die; I'm going to die; I'm going to die. The squealing sounds like a pig in pain. The burning pain is beyond; I feel faint again, it's too much. They should all be in jail and unable to walk around freely. They cannot put someone else through this; I don't know how I survived.

Why am I burning? I hear you bled, and they cleaned it up? I'm trying to make sense of what I'm hearing. Is it alcohol or alcohol solution? Would that burn? I don't know.

I google to understand. Alcohol that comes into direct contact with mucous membranes will immediately begin to irritate and break down those tissues. This is especially true of the vagina, which has very sensitive membranes throughout. Even one instance of this practice could result in damage to this sensitive sexual organ. You guys are absolute monsters, pure evil.

I now feel myself going back and forth whilst someone is inside of me. It's the first time I've heard myself say anything terrible to them; I f*cking hate you, I f*cking hate you; geez, that wasn't smart. Then I listen to myself again: I'm going to throw up. Seriously, I'm going to be sick. They say choke on your own spew bitch. I am so in tune with my higher self but still can't work everything out. I'm exhausted and think it's over for tonight, as I hear. Thank God that's over.

I remember going to see Lilith on her last birthday. It was July 1, 2023, and she still lived in Double Bay. By then, I was operating from a different dimension. The cup of tea I was holding was thrown towards her. Cleaning it up, I was so embarrassed and apologetic. I didn't understand, but my Soul did, and I gave her a peace bracelet. There won't be any peace where she's going.

Michelle Ashton

Sunday, 20th August 2023

Dear Journal,

I didn't get much sleep last night; I was in so much pain, and once again, I woke up crying my eyes out. Now I know why I feel a cut close to my vaginal opening. The mind is so powerful to block it all out. I always look to forgive; God cannot expect me to forgive this.

I keep grabbing my female bits, crying, and begging to please stop, please stop. I want this to stop now in 2023, before I would have turned to drugs to mask any unbearable pain, not this time, not ever. I will feel these emotions and work on finding out what's physically wrong with me; at least, I now understand what to tell the docs. I don't even know how to let a female doctor down there without crying; the thought is petrifying. I forking hate them so much, that I'm out of words to describe my hatred. The only thing I can think of is what I said in my last journal entry: the devil does have a face, or in this case, faces.

The squeals are terrifying. The noise resembles a painful, suppressed scream, and the pleading is unbearable to hear. Then I hear come here bitch, we're not finished. I ask when are you going to stop? How long is Ian away for? The squeals are so loud now; shut up bitch, if you make any more noise, you're really going to get it. I ask Spirit how long did this go on. I hear five hours. Fork, I feel so sick. It's no wonder I blocked this out for over a decade. Is my throat chakra blockage not from Ian but from the, shut up bitch? If you make any more noise, you're really going to get it. Is that why? Was I too scared to scream?

I can't deal with this; I need a break from my mind; I feel like mine is going to snap. The pain is unbearable, and then it gets so much worse. You like to see people suffer, and I get a flash of my fur baby Pucci. I hear myself scream, omg no no no no nooooooooooooooooooooooooooo. What's wrong with you, what's wrong with you. If I wasn't broken before, they just finished me off, they have ripped out my Soul.

I have decided not to give my new phone number to my mum and dad. I know they did their best, but I am standing my ground with everyone now, and their best wasn't good enough for me. I feel they failed me as parents; look at the life I lived. I know how bad I feel that I failed to protect Pucci, and I have to live with that, and they will have to live with their guilt, too. I'm not taking them into my next chapter. My brand-new life where I don't let anyone put shit on me, or put up with anything I'm uncomfortable with and I won't let things slide just to keep the peace.

It doesn't end here. Peter calls Ian In Bali. Ian isn't aware that Lilith and Andrew are involved. They say to Peter we have to live here. Why was Ian not more concerned when I was outside a month later when I shit myself? I can understand him thinking maybe it was better for me not to know the truth, but I was in a building with my perpetrators, not only that I trusted them. Fork, idiot, what a forking idiot. Is this why he moved into the spare room? I have always talked in my sleep; that must have been frightening to hear, especially knowing he had bought the apartment without my knowledge or consent, putting me in harm's way. He also could have helped with all the physical issues and the emotional scars. I'm going through all of this alone. I have never before called him stupid. That has never been a word that came to mind when I thought of him; it does now: stupid, foolish man. I bet those squeals and cries he heard in the middle of the night are a daily ritual where he's going.

This is a horror film that doesn't stop. I am now being shown this absolute barbaric pain around the ring of my vagina. My vagina is red raw. Here in Arncliffe, I put ice on, and it melts instantly. I can't make sense; I can't understand. What is going on? More information, please guides; everything is so fragmented. I'm in a bath, that stings to high Heaven. I can't tell what it is; I feel so sick. I hear wash yourself in that you dirty c*nt. Oh my gosh, I get it; I see the green bottle, it is Isocol, that's what my guides were trying to tell me about the alcohol; it's Isocol. The pain is too much, and I pass out again. Peter, and Andrew drag me out of the bath, one under each armpit; you're a heavy bitch, aren't you. I'm put on the bed. Andrew sticks his whole fist up me, cutting me with his watch; you bled on me, you dirty bitch. Lilith gets Isocol on a cotton ball and sticks it straight on the open cut to stop it bleeding. They are sticking all sorts of stuff up me. They put a condom on an object they bring in. I can't make it out; is it a rolling pin? I need the smallest clamp for a pap smear; no wonder the squeals. It's just forking barbaric. I'm squealing, please stop, please stop, please. I'm going to die, I'm going to die, you're going to kill me, you're going to kill me. Yeah, squeal, you f*cking pig. I don't know how I endured that and live to write in this journal.

I read that gastrointestinal, sexual and reproductive health problems are common physical symptoms of sexual assault. I had all three. I thought it came from the brain surgery, not torture and gang rape. I was suffering for years and still do; Ian saw me struggle. If I were run down or had any minor infection, I would pass so much wind. It was really embarrassing. I could have had a hole in my colon leaking into my stomach; these perforations can be fatal; it could have finished me off. I tried everything. Ian stood by, watched and never said a word. How was I married to such a monster? I'm so glad I didn't have kids with him. As long as I live, I never want to see his face again. Ian doesn't exist in my world. Maybe my mind can protect me from remembering that fifteen years of hell. Fork him, fork them; I hope they all get what's coming.

This horror film continues. They are banging the back of my head. I just had major brain surgery right there. They all knew where my massive tumour had just been removed. Are they trying to kill me, give me internal bleeding? What? What if I died right there in their apartment? Seriously, they are barbaric on a whole other level; I want to be sick now in 2023. I understand why I blocked this out. I probably would have died from shock if it was revealed to me then; my body was already weak from what I had just been through.

I hear a knock at the door; who else Is there? Oh no, I say, oh no. Please, please, please, I can't take anymore, bad luck bitch. How will anyone ever be able to knock at my door again? I keep hearing the knock, and I want to die. Why didn't God just take me right there and then? This is just beyond; I'm going to the police tomorrow. I hope they all get what they deserve.

I can't wait for the four of them to watch my comeback. I'm certain my life will be so magnetic they won't be able to help but see my light. Get your sunnies out, see you next Tuesday's!

Michelle Ashton

Monday, 21st August 2023

Dear Journal,

No sleep is the new norm. My cortisol must be running so high. I am meeting Salma at Mascot Police Station, but before I do, I must call Roses Only to see if they will be kind enough to delete my address from their records when Lilith and Andrew sent flowers for Pucci's passing. I also need to go into Shopify to set all products to zero. I would hate a bride buying and getting excited about her new dress. I couldn't let her down; I simply could not think about work right now. Getting through each day is a task in itself; showering and feeding myself whilst trying not to go completely nuts Is my priority.

I met Salma at the police station; I am so grateful she dropped everything to support me. It wasn't easy, but the police were very kind and caring. They have my journal notes, plus Ian, Andrew, and Lilith's contact details. They also know the couple own a property in Bali that my ex-husband sold to them. I wish I could be a fly on the wall when the cops arrive at their door. I'm sure they thought they had gotten away with this. Did they know there is no statute of limitations on reporting sexual assault? I hope they get their Karma and are haunted for Eternity.

I arrive home, and once again. It takes me a while. I need to make sure no one is behind me coming into the car park, and then I have to wait for the security gate to shut behind me. I get into the elevator, and a guy gets in. I stand as far away from him as possible. My heart is beating through my chest; I feel like I'm about to have a heart attack. After what felt like the longest ride in history, I finally made it to the fifth floor, but I did not put my key in the door until I saw the lift door close. I cannot live like this.

Once inside, the downloads continue. When Ian is called in Bali, I am talking to him. I say babe, please, please help me they are hurting me so bad, I love you, please help me. Then I screamed with pain; why doesn't he call the police or friends of mine to help? I don't understand. My wise guy is in jail; we are so close, that he would do anything for me. Ian knows this and has a friend's phone number to call in times of need, and used the number not long after my brain surgery to get out of a million-dollar debt. That was a financial matter handled for him because he was my husband. This was me, in real forking danger. I hate him so much; he mistreated me, and I continued loving him. I hope he rots in hell.

Michelle Ashton

Tuesday, 22nd August 2023

Dear Journal,

I saw my new doc today; what a way to start, poor woman. Doctor Hasan was very kind and patient whilst she explained everything to me in detail. I write some things down, as understandably, my brain is foggy. This bout of PTSD is a million times worse than the first one that was thought to be brought on from the brain surgery. I can't get my head around how I can still feel a cut near the vaginal opening. The doctor is very helpful and discussed that a cut consistently irritated by acidic urine is harder to heal without treatment; she also advised that a break would have healed, but arthritis can occur if fractures are not cared for properly. Doc has ordered an x-ray for my painful shoulder, and given me a referral for the gynaecologist at the Womans Health and research institute of Australia.

That was my morning, and I was so freaked out in the afternoon. I don't think I've ever been more scared in my entire life. For my last birthday, my brother shouted me and a group of my girlfriends to a decadent lunch in the city. Lilith was one of eight girls, and we had a WhatsApp group to share laughs and pictures from the night. I was warned by Salma, who is still a group member, that Lilith was asking if a friend would have a key to my house. WTF? Are you forking serious? Every time I get scared, I make that painful squealing sound that I was making on Horror Night. I have no idea how I will sleep for the next two nights. I'm getting an extra lock on my door Thursday; but right now, that feels like an Eternity away. I'll be lucky to make it through this in one piece. I know my body isn't in one piece, but I don't want my mind to follow suit. I must make my home feel safer until I get the extra lock. I already have an alarm, and coded door locks for the internal doors; now I have jammed things under the door and put furniture up against it to prevent it from opening; I've also put a big knife under my bed for extra peace of mind.

I am in so much pain tonight that I can't even sit in my chair. I'm not tired at all, but I am going to bed so I can lie down; I will read Angel Prayers, Harnessing the help of Heaven to Create Miracles. Ain't that the truth, Kyle Gray.

Michelle Ashton

Wednesday, 23rd August 2023

Dear Journal,

I manage a few hours of sleep, wake up, and think about this ordeal. When will I ever think of anything else or be able to make any sense of the fact that I wasn't able to have children and all the other physical symptoms, not to mention the emotional scars? I honestly have no idea; all I can concentrate on is today; it's too overwhelming. I'm not sure if I journaled this the other day, but I took a pen to a piece of paper and asked my guides what message they had for me; my hand-wrote

You will be ok
You will get through this
You are safe

I keep repeating this to myself over and over and only concentrate on putting one foot in front of the other, but I had no choice this morning; I had to deal with One Kiss. Before starting my label, I did a lot of research in the same industry. I owned a beautiful bridal boutique called Savvy Brides in Double Bay, a ritzy harbourside suburb of the eastern suburbs that is full of upscale boutiques, beauty salons, and restaurants. I was honoured to share such a special moment in many bride's lives. Helping them to choose that one dress that would take them from a Miss to a Mrs. Pinch me, what a privilege, and if that wasn't enough, the Australian Bridal Industry Academy rewarded me with winning the Best Bridal Boutique in my state. What a humbling acknowledgment.

To say I felt the love was a huge understatement. I know first-hand how long it takes to pick that one dress. It kills me to think of a beautiful bride-to-be, spending hours on my design tool, creating their perfect dress, showing their mum and bridesmaids and having their heart set on a dress they designed themselves, only to find that they can't purchase it. I can't bear the thought of hurting someone like that; I know how important this is to them; it's a dress that will live in their hearts and minds for a lifetime. I had to make the Soul-destroying decision to shut down my website. I only launched not even three months ago. Cael from Hello Spruce and I have just spent months designing, implementing, and perfecting it. The amount of detail in such an innovative design tool website is unfathomable. My knowledge of the bridal industry and Cael being a forward-thinking web genius made us a great team.

I am forever grateful for his incredible work and the kindness he showed when I messaged him, saying it was a serious matter and not to ask any questions. He did as I asked and took the burden off my back by shutting it down. Today, I could hardly tie my shoelaces, let alone try to achieve anything technical. Cael has a technical mind. I remember discussing web ranking with him one day, and he explained the difficulty of competing with the song One Kiss. That's where it all began, Cael; what a great song it is. That was my biggest dream for so many years. It's heartbreaking, but I have a new dream now: to live pain-free and in peace. That's my new dream. I have no idea how I will live. I have a few thousand in my apartment bank account, so I am ok for a bit, but I have no potential future earnings. I'm not even sure when I can return to my beautiful NDIS work or how to repay my brother for his loan to One Kiss. I have no idea about any of it, but I cannot think about the future for once. I need to concentrate on here and now. I know the Universe will take care of it. I don't know how, but I trust the Universe won't let me down; it has my back.

I take the website link off Instagram. I will leave the page there so my friends don't wonder what's happening. I don't want Lilith to think something is seriously wrong until the cops arrive at her door. I wish Spirit would give me the ability to see the look on her face when she realises that I have worked out that she is the devil. I'm trying to relax until my extra lock gets installed tomorrow, so I listen to my favourite song. Not many people know it's my favourite; I thought it wasn't cool enough; it's so cool. Freida knows my favourite song, as one day I was trying to cheer her up and asked her what her favourite was so I could play for her. Freida didn't know; I commented that it was okay and that we would listen to my favourite then. Magic by Olivia Newtown John, whom I have loved since her Grease days. My ex-husband knew many artists, but I was starstruck when I knew she was on the phone. The lyrics—woah, no wonder it's been my favourite for years.

  Come take my hand
You should know me
I've always been in your mind
You know I will be kind
I'll be guiding you

  Building your dream has to start now
There's no other road to take
You won't make a mistake
I'll be guiding you

  You have to believe we are magic
Nothin' can stand in our way
You have to believe we are magic
Don't let your aim ever stray
And if all your hopes survive, destiny will arrive
I'll bring all your dreams alive for you
I'll bring all your dreams alive for you

From where I stand, you are home free
The planets align, so rare
There's promise in the air
And I'm guiding you

Through every turn, I'll be near you
I'll come anytime you call
I'll catch you when you fall
I'll be guiding you

You have to believe we are magic
Nothin' can stand in our way
You have to believe we are magic
Don't let your aim ever stray
And if all your hopes survive, destiny will arrive
I'll bring all your dreams alive for you
I'll bring all your dreams alive for you

You have to believe we are magic
Nothin' can stand in our way
You have to believe we are magic
Don't let your aim ever stray
And if all your hopes survive, destiny will arrive
I'll bring all your dreams alive for you
I'll bring all your dreams alive for you

Freida now knows her favourite songs, and we have a playlist for her on my Spotify. I love her so much.

My mind is still racing, and I remember all sorts of things, including Lilith asking me if Ian could still get it up. I thought it was pretty crude, but that was Lilith. I believed she was referring to his age, but she obviously, had a front-row seat to what he saw or heard. I also remember our phone conversation right after I had shit myself; she was laughing, telling me how she went to Pilates and almost shit herself. I remember thinking how strange it was that it had just happened to me, but I said nothing, as obviously, it was a very embarrassing thing to happen at 36 years old. She knew I shit myself—forking disgrace of a woman. I just read that one does not have to operate with malice to do great harm; the absence of empathy is sufficient. Ain't that the bloody truth bitch. Once she saw what was going on, she did nothing to help me, and one of them was her long-term partner, twisted, forked-up people. I hope their hell is everything they deserve, and more.

I spoke to my brother and informed him about the website being taken down. I wanted to tell him that I would pay him back no matter what. I don't know how, but I will make it happen. Seb said the thought never crossed his mind, and it shouldn't be a concern of mine right now. He is so beautiful, and one of my top goals is to pay him back. I will make it happen, that's for sure; he believed in me. I will never forget his kindness, but I cannot concentrate on anything other than the basics right now. The first stop, is Service NSW, to change over the car's number plate. It's 1KISS, so it's very noticeable. I got a generic, inconspicuous plate in its place. Next up was a massive cleanout; I'm not selling anything more my ex-husband gave me that I hadn't already promised or consigned. I want nothing to do with him. Even though I could really do with the money. I don't want it; I don't want that energy. It was straight off to the charity bin downstairs. Designer clothes, bags, and shoes. This is so freeing. I am going to forget my whole time with him. Every single moment, even the brief, nice ones in between. It was all a lie, a huge forking horror story.

It's now 1.20 am, and I'm trying to get a little sleep before my 2nd visit to the police station in the morning. My guides want to give me more information before my appointment as the downloads continue. I now know why I said I'm going to throw up; seriously, I'm going to be sick and when they told me to choke on your own spew bitch. It's just beyond. I feel so sick right now; I think I will be sick here in 2023. No wonder on the night I was saying that. Revolting doesn't cut it. The stinging Isocol bath was the 2nd bath I was made to have. Firstly, I was put in a cold bath of about 30cm of water; I shake and freeze. Then they hang me over the front of the tub, one holding me, and another sticks something up my butt that makes me poo. Whilst I'm bathing in my own shit, Peter pulls his penis out and pees in the bath; Andrew then says yeah, I've gotta takes a piss too, and follows suit. They pull my arms to dangle over the sides, then say wash yourself in that you dirty c*nt.

I am left there whilst they go off for a while. I hear Lilith say we should make her drink it, and they come back with a glass, fill it up and hand it to me. My mouth is watering; I'm going to throw up. I love the gift of being able to feel things so deeply, but not when it comes to this stuff. I'm choking here in Arncliffe. Was I doing that on the night? How will I ever get that out of my head, making me bathe in my shit and then drink it, along with their piss? I have no words for their sick, twisted minds. I pray this is the last download; it's getting so revolting. I feel ill, and there is more information coming. It's not just degradation, torture, and gang rape; It's bloody attempted murder. They have a clear bag over my head, and whilst I'm gasping for breath, they take it on and off in intervals. I'm struggling to breathe. You're going to kill me; you're going to kill me. I'm going to die; I'm going to die; I'm going to die. Stop. Please stop.

Forking hell, they tried to kill me; what the fork? I almost died a few months before. What would they have done if they hadn't taken the bag off my head quickly enough? I was freaked out about the torture and gang rape. Thank you, guides, for not giving me all this information at once; it's too much. I can't believe they tried to kill me, and then Lilith and Andrew stayed friends with me for all these years. I need a break from everything and everyone.

Michelle Ashton

Thursday, 24th August 2023

Dear Journal,

Again, this morning, I went to the police station. I am blessed that my detective on the case is such a kind and caring woman. I was met at Mascot as she understood that I could not go to Bondi. I don't think I will ever be able to visit that suburb as long as I live. I was given the phone number for the NSW Police Sexual Violence Hotline, which

I can call 24/7. I'm so lucky to have this support free of charge. It's all so overwhelming, It's the worst nightmare I never wake up from. I keep repeating the advice from my guides.

   You will be ok
   You will get through this
   You are safe

Now I'm happier, the locksmith came. It wasn't an easy job, but the lovely guy persevered and got the job done. I can't remember the last time I felt so happy. I sent Salma a text message, and then, all of a sudden, I felt really tired. It was only 5 pm, and I thought I would lie down just for a moment. The next minute, my brother is phoning me; it's 9 pm. I never nap; I admire people who can do that. I must have finally felt safer; that's the most sleep I've had in days. Seb is asking for my wise guy's phone number. I know his heart is in the right place, but he needs to respect my decision and not have anything to do with my old life. That chapter is closed. I simply need to move out of that old energy. It's done, it's over, it's finished. New life, here I come. Bring it on; I'm all in.

I stuffed up the last part of my life with the decisions I made in the best interests of others. Decisions I make now are going to be in my best interests. What a beautiful feeling, what's best for Shell. Wow I'm not sure I've ever made decisions from that space. I was excited to pick a movie a few weeks back, and now I'm designing my whole life. I love that when I commit to something, I'm all In. I go for it; I just realised I found something about myself that I love, and that makes me so happy. One day at a time, maybe tomorrow I will find another and the next day, and so on.

  Michelle Ashton

Friday, 25th August 2023

Dear Journal,

When will I wake up, and Horror Night is not the first thing on my mind? I hate them all. Instead of my days filled with beach mornings, meditation, gym, sunshine, and work that I love, it's filled with tears and driving to Galston for holistic counselling, and Reiki sessions. I bought a car seat cushion to make the drive more comfortable. I was getting ready, drying my hair, when I got a flashback; now I understand why my hair wasn't wet.

Then I walked into my loungeroom, which is still set up as an office. I'll get onto that tomorrow; that will be tough, to say the least. In my little dining area, I only have one occasional chair. I eat on it, read, and watch my tiny TV monitor. It was used for everything, but then I remembered Ian paid for it, down to the rubbish it went. I don't need a forking thing from him; I'd rather sit on the floor; anything to do with his energy is repulsive. Next up was a text message to my brother.

Hey just so you know, I never want to have that conversation again about Les. Everything I do is going to be the right thing &

I want you to do that too, I beg you do not do anything that isn't right. Karma always comes so please learn from my experience. I deleted his contact so I don't have to have that conversation ever again or feel bad about my boundaries I set, It's done. I love you so much & I only want good things for you. talk later x

On the way to Galston, I stop at Castle Hill Towers for a ring clip for my new key. I saw the newsagent before me and bought a ticket for next week's 40 million Powerball. I don't need that much money, but it would be nice to hand over my journal entries for someone to make into a book so I can finally have a voice and clear this throat chakra.

Before returning home, I went to the Supa Centre in Moore Park. I spent some of my much-needed savings on a coffee table; I haven't had one in almost two years, to say I'm looking forward to the delivery Is an understatement. I need every cent to go towards living and medical expenses, but I have complete faith in the Universe. I will have a meditation cushion and a little coffee table for my cuppa. That made me smile.

Michelle Ashton

Saturday, 26th August 2023

Dear Journal,

I awoke early after having a bizarre dream about Peter and a moth, but I am struggling to get out of bed, as I know what awaits me. Today, I'm packing up my One Kiss dream. I put my big girl panties on and got to work. I came across the kiss shoes that were bought for the launch shoot. It was both a sweet and sad memory. It was tough for me to keep it together that day. That morning, Adonis and I had the text argument when he blocked me. It went like this: I sent him my welcome to today meditation.

> *Me: Good morning I know you won't get this until you take off DND smart, I do that too so I don't get rat bags waking me up. Im in the best mood ever!!!!*
> *Today is the day I get to see all my years of hard work come together. Your on hols so you have plenty of time it's a nice way to start your day!*
> *Hope your having the best time, touch base when your back & tell me about your trip!!*
>
> *Noah: Pls no more messages! I deed space! For a reason! Thank u.*
>
> *Me: All good Noah, no one is raining on my parade today!! Enjoy your trip!!*
>
> *Noah: Not all about u?*
>
> *Me: Im not getting into this, I know its not, Im not self absorbed!!*
> *Please today is a very important & special day for me... Years & years of blood sweat & tears hopefully all comes together*

Noah: Pls leave me alone!

Me: Ditto!

Noah: I'm blocking u

Me: How lovely

Noah: U don't listen or respect my boundaries! So........

Truer words have never been spoken. No one was raining on my parade. I stopped replying; I was trying to stay positive. I had worked so hard to see it all come together and my vision come to life. Konstantina was waiting for me; I didn't have time for that rubbish. Konstantina Mittas didn't have a title, but it should have been Guardian Angel. She is an expert in the fashion industry, a master of her field, and she took me under her wing. Kon created the dream team, which comprised the best of the best.

Behind the scenes was the incredibly talented pattern and dressmaker Leonardo. He also does work for Camilla and wedding dresses for Steven Kahlil; they are some very lucky brides. Then, she had Viva Vayspap as the fabulous artistic stylist for the shoot. Viva and Kon often work together, and it shows. They got my vibe and ran with it, exceeding my expectations. It was creative madness, and I loved it. As the exceptionally gifted make-up artist, Elsa Morgan nailed the looks in no time. Next up, she enticed the most accomplished photographer, Julie Adams, to do my shoot. Julie has such high-profile clients, and Kon got her to work on our little start-up label. Pinch me, and because of Julie's calibre, we got to choose some highly skilled, beautiful models from IMG that would never have come to a casting for an unknown label. Kon didn't stop there. She managed to lure the absolute best in his field, the most creative videographer, Sam Hastwell. What a talented man. Last but not least, my favourite, John Pulitano, the superstar hairdresser. Johnny is exceptionally gifted and travels the world styling hair. He was so humble to sit in a studio in Alexandria for two days, free of charge. What a special Soul; how did I get so blessed?

Love, Michelle Ashton

Sunday, 27th August 2023

Dear Journal,

Wow, I slept in until 8.30 am. I can't remember the last time I slept in. The counsellor says it will be up and down; recovery isn't a straight line, so I'm just being kind to myself and taking it day by day. I'm continuing my big clean out and see the bathroom scales. There was a time when I used to weigh myself every day, but I haven't in forever. I kept them to weigh dresses for postage. I just looked at them and thought they don't bring me joy; off to charity, they go. I can't imagine never knowing what I weigh; it's so liberating. Why do we put all this pressure on ourselves, especially women? It's insanity to think how perfect we strive to be when beauty lies within.

My phone rings, It's Salma, she checks on me, multiple times per day. What a beautiful Soul. I told her that I think Ian should have had a duty of care to share his information so I could get proper medical care. There should be a law for that; not only did he not report a crime, he let me live with such bad gastrointestinal issues that any slight infection or eating the wrong foods would cause a flare-up. He just watched on and didn't say a word. I remember a time in Bondi when I ate an ice cream, and my stomach swelled so much. I looked like I was nine months pregnant. I had the worst abdominal pain, was sweating profusely, crying, and begging him to help me, to take me to the hospital. The pain was so unbearable. He handed me Gaviscon tablets. I was still in pain hours later; the sheets were soaking wet, and I thought it must have been dairy, so that went on to my massive list of things I didn't eat. Hiding that information from me was extremely dangerous; I could have died. Google states "The law says we all have a duty of care to take reasonable care not to cause foreseeable harm to other people or their property. This is also known as the law of negligence." Forking arsehole.

Next up, I got some much-needed housework done. I had let everything go. I was cleaning the toilet and using different organic wipes than other parts of the bathroom, then I thought, does it bloody matter? I've drank shit and piss water. I'm not sure that thought will ever leave my mind. To stop thinking, I put on Spotify. I choose an easy-listening playlist. One of Freida's favourite songs starts playing. I love

Peace Train by Yusuf / Cat Stevens. I thought I hadn't heard her playlist for a while; I'll pop it on. The song that played made me drop to the floor in a prayer pose. I thank God for Freida being in my life; that is no coincidence. The lyrics to her favourite song I Am Woman by Helen Reddy.

> I am woman, hear me roar
> In numbers too big to ignore
> And I know too much to go back an' pretend
> 'Cause I've heard it all before
> And I've been down there on the floor
> No one's ever gonna keep me down again
>
> Whoa, yes, I am wise
> But it's wisdom born of pain
> Yes, I've paid the price
> But look how much I've gained
> If I have to, I can do anything
> I am strong (strong)
> I am invincible (invincible)
> I am woman (ooh)
>
> You can bend but never break me
> 'Cause it only serves to make me
> More determined to achieve my final goal
> And I come back even stronger
> Not a novice any longer
> 'Cause you've deepened the conviction in my soul

Oh, yes, I am wise
But it's wisdom born of pain
Yes, I've paid the price
But look how much I've gained
If I have to, I can do anything
I am strong (strong)
I am invincible (invincible)
I am woman (ooh)

I am woman, watch me grow
See me standing toe to toe
As I spread my lovin' arms across the land
But I'm still an embryo
With a long, long way to go
Until I make my brother understand

Whoa yes, I am wise
But it's wisdom born of pain
Yes, I've paid the price
But look how much I've gained
If I have to, I can face anything
I am strong (strong)
I am invincible (invincible)
I am woman
I am woman (I am woman)
I am invincible (I am woman), I am strong
I am woman (I am woman)
I am invincible (I am woman), I am strong
I am woman (I am woman)
I am woman (I am woman)

Freida is part of my Soul family, that's for sure. It's now the evening, and I was guided to write the ending of my journal. How would I like it to end? You are probably wondering what happened with Adonis and me. In July, I bought two tickets to Elvis the Musical, which will be playing in September at the State Theatre in Sydney. I go with Salma and see him there. I've missed that perfect face. He looks even more beautiful than I remember. I love that man so much, but I try to be cool. I go to introduce him. Salma this is Adonis, Adonis this is Salma. Oh my gosh, that wasn't cool. I've been used to calling him that for months; I forget to call him Noah. You think I would be more embarrassed, but I'm not; that man will someday be my husband. By the way, we won't have a prenup. I would never do what my ex did to me. Anyway, who needs an exit strategy when it's forever?

Back to tonight, I got lost in that perfect moment. It's 10.30, and I'm ready for bed; since I got the extra door lock on, I have gotten tired and slept a little better. I must have been running on adrenaline. I also have an early start with Ridly, the removal guys; they will take away all the office stuff to sort for recycling, except the fabrics that I want to donate. I was guided to a place that sounded perfect. The Sewing Basket in Caringbah is run by Achieve Australia. They have been providing services to support people with disability since 1952. Donations and volunteers run the sewing shops. I have so much gratitude. I love to help in any way I can; now, I just have to borrow my brother's truck and his muscles to drop them all off. I can't believe this all fit in here. How did It? I suppose it didn't; I used to push the fabrics down to sit to eat and then back up to work. Suddenly, it hit me: I will call it One Kiss when I turn my journal notes into a book. I always knew it would be a huge success. I didn't envision helping others through my love and pain, but I am so proud of myself for finding a way to make my One Kiss dream a reality.

Love, Michelle Ashton

Monday, 28th August 2023

Dear Journal,

Ridly Rubbish Removal came, and I almost had a heart attack at the quote: $2,700 + GST for a full truck of mixed waste. They can't recycle everything, but they sort through it and try to recycle what they can. My local council, Bayside, has four free clean-up days a year, and today is the day. Inspite of that, I thought Shell, we all need to do our part, by not sending everything straight to landfill, but geez Louise, I don't even have a job. I thought spending a few hundred on a beautiful coffee table was a lot in my current financial position. I just have to keep believing what I know to be true: you do good, and good will come to you. I transferred some much-needed dollars to pay the expensive recycling bill. I'm being good to our planet, and I know the Universe appreciates my efforts.

I started chatting with Salma about the high price of rubbish removal. I said most people wouldn't pay more, especially if they were in my shoes, so something needs to change to make it easier to help the planet. Salma asks why it costs so much. Once they return to the recycling depot, each item needs to be sorted; it's very labour-intensive. Salma came up with a great idea: the prisoners should do it, and hopefully, it would also help them to become more empathetic towards our planet. I think that's a great idea, Salma.

Afterwards, I was quietly sitting in my empty lounge room. I heard an old friend's voice; it was as clear as day, like she was sitting right beside me, "Oh, she's just a crazy bitch." Hearing that was really disappointing; we were extremely close. I will just chalk that up to a drug-fuelled night, and I'm the crazy one? What a blessing it is to have this gift to hear things the Divine wants or needs me to, but I will have to learn to ignore any negative energy and always be in the presence of love. Speaking about the presence of love, God loves me, that's for sure. I have heard that God uncovers gifts for you on the journey. I was so happy with the gift of compassion. Guess what else?

Oh, my gosh!!!!!!!!!!!!!! I'm a writer!!!!!!!!!!!!!! I don't need to give my journal notes to anyone; I can do it myself. It flows so easily; it must be a past-life connection. Who was I? In this lifetime, I wasn't great at school; I've had to get help with copywriting, I type with one hand, and I haven't even read one book in its entirety. Wow, what an incredible magical Universe we live in. Seriously, pinch me. Thank you, Universe. Thank you. Thank you. I feel so blessed. I won't tell anyone. It's going to be so hard, especially with Seb, Salma, and Reiki Angel. They all know I journal; they have read pieces. Unfortunately, the police know, too; they have a section in my file. All this time, I thought I was journaling for therapeutic reasons. What a surprise for my loved ones. I'd be the last person they would expect to write a book. Then I hear words from my favourite song. You have to believe we are magic.

I am then guided to Google how many Twin Flames become writers, and Katy's review comes up. I screenshot it, and the time is 11.11. This Angel number is considered to be powerful and creative, signifying that you are in alignment with Divine guidance and representing new beginnings, leadership, and Spirituality. I will never underestimate how magical our Universe is.

Quora - Katy updated - aug 12

If this was not an extremely emotional journey, no one would be writing about it. No one can tell anyone how to "be" with their twin flame. We are all learning as we go along. I have learned that it is not about being with your twin flame as in the ego based 3D relationship template. In fact, this is an energetic connection with a soul that is an exact vibrational match, this energy is so powerful to activate the bubble love experience, a love experience that transcends all knowing, the heart chakra flies wide open, you experience an out of this world intense energy attraction that defies anything you have ever experienced. It is intense. You don't even have to touch the person to experience this because it is about an exact energy match, this is why it transcends any and all other attractions you have ever had. So intense that most human beings can not handle it and they run from it. Most twin flames are not together as a couple, this is not the purpose of this heart love activation. I have learned and accepted that this is about activating that pure love that is from the heavens to the planet. I have come to realize this is what twin flames that are on the planet at the same time came to do. They are planted all around the globe and they feel the activation from miles and miles away and thus that intense GOD LOVE frequency is spread around.

After that heartfelt read, I listened to music, whilst eating my veggie soup. Red Hot Chili Peppers came on, and I thought back to the concert night in February. It really feels like a lifetime ago, but it was only just over six months. I got up to have a little dance in my vast lounge room. Oh my gosh, I felt like a little dance. YES!

Love, Michelle Ashton

Tuesday, 29th August 2023

Dear Journal,

I just woke up from the most moving dream; I was so touched. I told Salma that when I win the Powerball on Thursday, I can give a hefty portion to charity and tick off the 2nd goal on my list. It's not how I envisioned, but the Universe has bigger dreams than we ever could. Then I walked into my lounge room, opened the blinds and was reminded I had a perfect view.

The clean-up continued. I got rid of my tiny monitor because it only worked with Apple TV. I remembered Ian had one lying around, and decided to give it to me as a housewarming gift. I didn't want anything from him, so I discarded it. I prefer to listen to music anyway. The monitor had left some significant holes from the big screws I had taken out. I thought I'd have to go to Bunnings Hardware and get that stuff; what's that putty shit. Then I heard you weren't a handyman in a past life. My guides have a sense of humour.

On the way to the hardware, which isn't far, the pain is excruciating, some days are better than others. I'm sitting in the traffic, which isn't great anytime, but I'm usually more patient. It's hard to be happy when you're in pain. I pray that my birthday weekend at the serene and tranquil Bawley Ridge in Termeil will be a pain-free three-hour drive; you never know, and it's only under a month away.

Being unhappy is a vicious cycle; if we stay in the energy of unhappiness, the Universe will give us more to be unhappy about. The Universe doesn't understand we don't want it; it just matches our vibration, so I have to try even harder on days like today. I am so thankful I was still in block-out mode for all those long trips to the Central Coast, taking Freida to see her mum in the nursing home. I am happy that she spent so much time with her beautiful mother before she went to Heaven to hang out with the other Angels.

Love, Michelle Ashton

Wednesday, 30th August 2023

Dear Journal,

How can I forget when photo memories pop up on my phone? They were from a Bali holiday in early April 2018. Ian and I often hung out with Lilith and Andrew as he sold them an apartment in the same complex as our penthouse in Como Hotel Canggu, which they still own. Ian's daughter took us to a Japanese restaurant, where I got sick. I had an infection, and because of my immune issues, I was finding it hard to recover. Back in Sydney, I returned to work at my bridal boutique . I was so bloody tired, but I thought it was just the lack of sleep, I don't sleep well on the night flights home from Bali.

On Saturday night, after working all day, I had a friend's, hens night at a private home in Vaucluse, a prestigious suburb of Sydney. I was really tired but wanted to be there to celebrate with my close mate for her bachelorette. I thought I'd be ok after a champagne and a couple of lines. As the night went on, it didn't seem to matter how many lines of coke I had; I just got more and more tired. I was feeling so sick I had to go home. The Uber arrived, and the host, another friend, walked me out; just as we took off, she yelled out "Thanks for popping off." I had been in block-out mode, and that comment snapped me out of it. I have never been so mortified in my entire life. I had been passing smelly gas all over the party.

Many so-called friends were there, including Noah's ex-wife, and not one of them pulled me aside to check if I was okay. Clearly, I wasn't, or they could have called my ex-husband to pick me up. Plenty of the girls had his phone number, as we were all part of the same friend group. Nope, nothing, not a thing; who needs enemies? I never spoke about this with anyone, including my ex-husband, who I'm sure would have heard the rumours about his wife's fall from grace. I had never been more embarrassed in my entire life. I was then so vigilant with food that it had become the enemy. I would try foods at home with such trepidation, and if they didn't affect me. I would eat the same couple of things over and over. I would never try new foods if I were out. I went to the same lunch place for years, eating the identical meal as the day before. I kept my eating disorder a secret, and in the eastern suburbs, where being stick thin isn't out of the ordinary, along with my fake breasts, it mostly went unnoticed. I did have a couple of friends who asked if I was anorexic, but I just laughed and made excuses for my weight loss, just like anyone hiding an eating disorder.

My ex should have been helping me with everything, including the financial aspects; he could afford it. I just have to trust the Universe will provide me with the right people and financial assistance to live as pain-free as possible. I trusted him so much; others say he is ruthless; that's probably how he did so well at Virgin alongside Richard Branson. He was so proud of the fact that he was in his book. Now he is in another. Remembering everything is all just too much. My ex-husband could have helped me but stood by and watched me suffer. He is a bigger monster than the three arseholes from Horror Night. I called the caring detective and told her I couldn't proceed with the investigation at this stage; she agreed that my mental health was more important and would keep my case file for when I was stronger in the future.

After a really tough day, I got the best news. God answered one of my prayers. I pray daily for Seb's happiness, and he is ecstatic as he tells me he is getting married. I adore his fiancé, Isabella; she is such a beautiful girl inside and out, sweet and down to earth. Like me, she has a colourful past, but that's a bonus in my book as I believe it can give us more depth and compassion. They are so in love, and it's beautiful to witness; that's what life is all about, LOVE.

Love, Michelle Ashton

Note added 6th October 2024

This is my proudest entry. With the support of his beautiful wife, yes, that's right, Seb and Bella were married on 23-11-23 at my favourite church in Port Douglas. At the time, when they chose St Marys by the Sea, they had no idea of my adoration. That was just another sign that they were meant for each other. On the 1st March 2024, Seb contacted the Public Drug Rehabilitation of the SESLHD and now lives a quiet, drug-free life in the country, relatively quiet, with their two dogs and my beautiful niece and nephew there as often as possible. Bella treats my brother like a king and the kids as her own. I smile from ear to ear while writing this, knowing God has answered my prayer.

Love, Michelle Ashton

Thursday, 31st August 2023

Dear Journal,

This morning, I got such disappointing news. The sonographer has Covid and has called in sick, so my tests must be rescheduled. I am sad but remain kind; it's not anyone's fault. I told the receptionist I hope the staff member gets better real soon. As It is an internal ultrasound, I am requesting a woman sonographer. The next available appointment is on the 11th of September. I'm really disappointed; I wanted the results to work out how to feel better. Now that I'm a writer, I have no other option except to sit, but then I think I've waited over a decade, so what's another couple of weeks? I'll read Breathe Magazine instead. I am relaxing on my meditation cushion, and only a couple of pages in when I see a quote from Oprah Winfrey: "Know what sparks the light in you so that you, in your own way, can illuminate the world." I absolutely love it. That's easy, Oprah; helping others sparks the light in me.

Love, Michelle Ashton

Friday, 1st September 2023

Dear Journal,

I have woken up feeling numb. I must remember the counsellor's words: recovery will be up and down; it isn't a straight line. I'm feeling so overwhelmed by how much there is to process. I am in utter disbelief anyone, let alone your husband, would let another person suffer when they could have helped; that's not humanity. I then thought of all the health issues I've had to deal with whilst with Ian.

- Brain surgery
- PTSD
- Eye problems, including a scar on my left pupil
- Headaches & fatigue
- Depression
- Cognitive & memory issues
- Dehydration
- Jaw pain
- Throat issues
- Tonsillectomy
- Palatal myoclonus
- Sleep issues
- Tinnitus
- Overactive bladder
- Central nervous system problems
- Hair loss
- Bruising easily
- Osteopenia
- High copper levels
- Balance issues
- Broken calcaneus
- Premature menopause & related issues
- Digestive & gastrointestinal problems
- Allergies, including anaphylaxis

Shoulder, wrist & inner thigh pain
Pelvic & anal pain
Eating disorder
Immune issues
Pericarditis

Everything after the brain surgery, I was led to believe, had stemmed from that. How do I ever process, that I will never know? I honestly wonder how I'm still alive, and now I can add torture, gang rape and attempted murder to my very long list. I was then guided to google renal blunt trauma complications, and I found these are things I have suffered.

Anemia
Weak bones and increased risk of bone fractures
Decreased Immune
Reduced Fertility
Pericarditis
Damage to your central nervous system

I have never hated anyone before now. If someone wasn't my cup of tea I would just say I wasn't fond of them. I forking hate Ian and those arseholes from Horror Night. I do not know how to move forward; I have so much to process. Since I was not waiting for the police to knock on Lilith and Andrew's door anymore, it didn't matter that friends got suspicious, so I shut down my Instagram profile. Building such a strong following took years of hard work and dedication. I don't care anymore. I have nothing left in the tank.

I take a few screenshots as memories. I need to take care of my mental health. I need all my strength to move forward; @onekissbabe is permanently deleted.

Michelle Ashton

Saturday, 2nd September 2023

Dear Journal,

It started as a good day, but then I received sickening information about the second so-called robbery in Tamarama. Ian was the one who hid the jewellery; he was tired of Peter hanging around and blamed him. I honestly can't deal with this latest download; all this happened to me because of my ex-husband's lies and dishonesty. He is the biggest see you next Tuesday on Earth. Nothing will stop me from releasing this book and being able to clear my throat chakra. Not even the fact that I didn't win the Powerball. I will find another way. Over the years, Ian has witnessed my fierce determination, and this is a win-win. I will finally have a voice, and help make a difference in the world.

Love, Michelle Ashton

Sunday, 3rd September 2023

Dear Journal,

Salma and I were discussing the Blue Zone areas around the world and how much food plays a part in our longevity. I think it also has a significant impact on our quality of life. Now that I have changed my ways of eating, my allergies are basically non-existent. It is so refreshing. I was always awfully restricted. Since switching to a plant-based diet, I eat whatever I want, and more than I ever have in my life. I love food and animals; they are not the same thing.

Love, Michelle Ashton

Note added 9th October 2024

I would tolerate eating vegetarian meals when dining out if restaurants didn't have a vegan option. I last had to do this at a fancy degustation restaurant almost a year ago for my brother and Bella's wedding. I am very proud of my vegan lifestyle, and I will no longer support animal cruelty. Companies and restaurants need to respect that each of us is entitled to live our lives however we wish. I think it's discrimination not to offer an alternative.

Monday, 4th September 2023

Dear Journal,

This is a nightmare that I never wake up from. I do not want anything to do with my old life. I'm not surprised I blocked this out for so long. I couldn't have handled it; how clever are our minds? I can hardly cope now; I'm drug-free, and it's 2023. I don't know what comes over me; my higher self is always leading the way these days, and I am happy to let it. It's doing much better these last months than I had done for years. I pick up my phone and go through all my old contacts, deleting them one by one. I'm not sure why, but I do it, and before I know it, they are all gone.

I was then in tears when Michael Buble's song I'll Never Not Love You played. It is so beautiful, but the realisation set in. How will I ever trust anyone again? I was married to the devil. Speaking of devils, the downloads continued. I can't even write about it; it's really that bad, so disgusting and degrading. I can hardly breathe and can't even walk a step without dropping to my feet and wailing. I need this to stop, please, Divine, please. I know what I need to, enough. Peter, Andrew, and Lilith are not human. There is simply no other explanation. I am not coping in the slightest. I will write this book to clear my throat chakra and help humanity. Then, I will live the rest of my life in peace. That's what I need and deserve. I've had enough hardships. This week, I will step out of my comfort zone. As scary as some tasks seem, I will achieve as much as possible whilst remembering to be kind to myself. I can feel my psychic abilities strengthening daily, and I don't want to waste another moment living in fear.

Michelle Ashton

Tuesday, 5th September 2023

Dear Journal,

I've woken up in a fantastic mood today. After the downloads yesterday, nothing can hurt me that much ever again. I have suffered the worst of the worst. I am going to be unstoppable, mate. Watch out, world. So much has been taken from me. I will not allow anyone or anything, especially fear, to hold me back. I will live the rest of my life to the fullest and check off every goal. Bring it on, baby! I need to start with the little things; understandably, I have let things slip away. My E-Toll account is suspended, so I had to log in to pay; I found that my account says Mrs Michelle Ashton-Duffell. That makes me cry. I'm not a Mrs, and I want to forget that I was ever married. I believe in God. I shouldn't have to be a divorcee under these conditions. I wish it could be cleared from the records. I never want to be reminded of being married to that man. It's too terrifying. He is the devil. I have to change my name, I cannot have any reminders. I'm getting my divorce records to start the complex process. I'm waiting, waiting, waiting for the family law to answer the phone; the whole thing is so triggering. When will this end? Please answer the phone; it's only the first step. I am told to log into the Commonwealth Courts Portal. I can't even put the password in correctly; I'm seriously losing the plot. I want this nightmare to be over. When I finally log in, I'm reminded of the binding financial agreement Ian coerced me into signing. We were together for 15 years, and after everything he put me through, he also wanted to cheat me out of what I should have been entitled to. I hate him, and I want to die. I can't even have a change of name. I am stuck with that arseholes surname.

I was born Michelle Anne Ashton; then my mother changed my surname to my dad's. When I was old enough, I changed it back to Ashton. Then, at Ian's suggestion, I deleted Anne, as it was the same middle name of his ex-wife. I was then married and became Michelle Duffell, and sometime after, I had to complete a change of name to become my current name, Michelle Ashton-Duffell. I'm at my limit for a change of names. WTF, it's not like they are all completely different. I feel sick; how can I be stuck with that arses name, seriously? I have never been so disgusted by a name; what a horrible reminder. Please, let me have my name back. I want nothing to do with that man. Nothing, nothing, nothing.

It now gets worse; I'm having a panic attack. This is forking way too much. Breathe, Michelle, breathe, just breathe. I need to get this down in case something happens to me. If I die, my brother needs to find my journal notes and release them. Ian cannot get away with this. Whilst living in Bondi, I discovered I had high copper levels. The doctors couldn't work out why. They went through everything with me. What kind of taps did I have at home? All that I was eating and drinking. My prescription medicine and vitamin supplements. They could not find a reason. I started having infra-red saunas to reduce the levels; it became very costly, so I got one for home to use regularly.

After I survived brain surgery, and then Horror Night. Ian decides, I'm no use to him anymore. He doesn't want to have sex with me. I won't be the mother of his child; I'm just costing him money. I see him go to the pantry where I keep my vitamin supplements and swap over the bottle. The contents inside didn't match the BioCeuticals label, so the doctors didn't pick it up. I was ingesting these daily. That's why I was guided to throw them out not long ago. The Divine was once again getting me ready for what was coming. They have always been a step ahead. I asked why he hadn't just left me. I hear he thought everyone would think he was a complete arse after I had just made it through brain surgery. How am I still alive? He tried to kill me. Is this why I have neurological problems? This is way too much. It's all so sick and twisted that it doesn't seem real; how is this my life? It's like a Steven Spielberg movie.

I think about some of Ian's illegal activities.

He surrendered his green card before getting investigated for tax fraud by the US government. Insurance fraud on a burglary at 30 Derby St, Vaucluse. Australian tax fraud on two Bali properties. One was sold, with a deal worked out between him and his mate Saxon Looker who was involved with the next project. Saxon then declared that he was owed one million dollars; Ian said he was a con man, and my friends helped him out of that debt.

The next project Sea Sentosa, Ian sold an apartment at mates rates to Lilith and Andrew. Then, it mysteriously ran out of money. He then brokered a deal with another mate of his, Malaysian billionaire businessman Ong Beng Seng. Sea Sentosa was then rebranded as a worldwide hotel chain, Como Hotels and Resorts, and Lilith and Andrew still own the same property. Ian then sold his multimillion-dollar Como Uma Canggu penthouse and received the funds into a Bali Commonwealth Bank account he had set up. The Commonwealth Bank also has branches in Australia, so he used the Commonwealth Bank card in Sydney to take out funds, bit by bit, to avoid being flagged, and paying taxes. He didn't declare this to his high-profile accountant, Bell Partners.

Next, Ian got involved in another company, IOT Group, but this time, it was publicly listed, and more challenging to have dodgy dealings, but still found a way. The Australian Federal Police searched our home. This company also mysteriously ran out of funding, ceased trading, and was removed from the Australian Stock Exchange. I know there are companies I've missed, so I Googled his Wikipedia profile to find many are removed, and he has updated it.

Ian knew many people in high places and thought I was just some stupid girl he had met in a massage parlour. He picked the wrong woman to fork with. I have God on my side, and he saw everything. The last download would have killed me in the past, but I'm not that girl anymore. I am strong, I am invincible, I am woman, and determined to rebuild my life. Ian's part in my book is over. When I decided to cut him out of my life a while back, Salma said it's your book, and he isn't in the next chapter. That gives me chills. Does she have psychic abilities, too? So yes, Salma, Ian isn't coming into my new chapter in any way, shape or form. No air time from me in my life or my thoughts. It's my book, and that man is dead to me.

Michelle Ashton

Wednesday, 6th September 2023

Dear Journal,

My new chapter started with seeing Virginia from Natural Beginnings. I was guided to her for holistic pelvic care a while back. The Divine knew I would need her and is always working in my favour, having me a step ahead every time. If I hadn't seen her and felt comfortable, the appointment would have been unbearable, as it was the hardest thing I've ever done. I found the strength and courage to open the door to my new life and make it through the 90-minute session. Thank goodness Virginia is such a nurturing Soul. I felt so vulnerable, even showering myself down there is scary. Towards the end of the session, she moved to my feet, lightly touching them. I got so scared I shook and ripped off the eye pillow. I apologise; she is so sweet. I didn't mean to scare her. When Virginia moved to my head, I felt so overwhelmed, and the strangest thing happened: as she performed a Buddhist chant, I saw myself leave my body, hovering above. Is this what happened on Horror Night? Did I disassociate?

When the session was over, I had never felt more exhausted in my whole life. The thirty-minute drive from Caringbah South felt like the biggest mission. I drove 50 in an 80 zone; cars swerved all around me. The steering wheel was hard to hold; I had no energy. I have never felt exhaustion like that. I had more energy after my six-hour brain tumour operation. I eventually made it home, got out of the car, and whilst trying to get my arm through the cardigan, I screamed, let me go! When I finally made it upstairs and went to the bathroom, peeing was so painful. I was then freezing and had to put on so many layers; no matter what I put on, I couldn't get warm; was I in shock? I just lay on my floor, in the direction that my back wasn't to the door. I continued to lie there, completely exhausted and kept reading my mirror. I had transferred my higher self's words. You will be ok, you will get through this, you are safe. Is that how I should have felt after Horror Night? But I just blocked it out and went to bed like nothing had happened. Fork, the mind is so powerful.

Michelle Ashton

Thursday, 7th September 2023

Dear Journal,

I could hardly sleep last night. I kept having a vision of a long, scissor-type instrument. I couldn't work out what it was, and then it came to me: Oh my gosh, it was nose clippers. They put nose clippers in my bottom. WTF? When will these visions ever stop?

Later, when I was going to see Reiki Angel, I listened to Bon Jovi; I love that band. I thought about when I saw Jon Bon Jovi coming out of an LA hotel. I was absolutely beside myself and asked him for a picture. I'm sure he gets bombarded with that request so many times a day, but the kind man obliged and let me get my fan pic; I treasure it. A song I'd never heard before came on: We Weren't Born To Follow. I listened to it about ten times in a row. The lyrics spoke to me like nothing I've heard in my entire life. It should be the song for all of humanity. It's now at the top of my favourites list; the lyrics couldn't be more perfect.

> This one goes out to the man who mines for miracles
> This one goes out to the ones in need
> This one goes out to the sinner and the cynical
> This ain't about no apology
> This road was paved by the hopeless and the hungry
> This road was paved by the winds of change
> Walking beside the guilty and the innocent
> How will you raise your hand when they call your name?
> Yeah, yeah, yeah

We weren't born to follow
Come on and get up off your knees
When life is a bitter pill to swallow
You gotta hold on to what you believe
Believe that the sun will shine tomorrow
And that your saints and sinners bleed
We weren't born to follow
You gotta stand up for what you believe
Let me hear you say yeah, yeah, yeah, oh yeah

This one's about anyone who does it differently
This one's about the one who cusses and spits
This ain't about our livin' in a fantasy
This ain't about givin' up or givin' in
Yeah, yeah, yeah

We weren't born to follow
Come on and get up off your knees
When life is a bitter pill to swallow
You gotta hold on to what you believe
Believe that the sun will shine tomorrow
And that your saints and sinners bleed
We weren't born to follow
You gotta stand up for what you believe
Let me hear you say yeah, yeah, yeah, oh yeah

Let me hear you say yeah, yeah, yeah, oh yeah

We weren't born to follow
Come on and get up off your knees

When life is a bitter pill to swallow
You gotta hold on to what you believe
Believe that the sun will shine tomorrow
And that your saints and sinners bleed
We weren't born to follow
You gotta stand up for what you believe
Let me hear you say yeah, yeah, yeah, oh yeah

Let me hear you say yeah, yeah, yeah, oh yeah

We weren't born to follow, oh yeah
(Yeah, yeah, yeah, oh yeah)
We weren't born to follow, oh yeah

I have a knowing; I don't know how, I just do. I get the feeling Adonis and I are a part of something huge. A movement? One Kiss movement. I couldn't be more grateful to be helping to carry out God's work; what a blessing. I smile from ear to ear when I write this. Watch out, world; Adonis and I will make a difference.

Love, Michelle Ashton

Friday, 8th September 2023

Dear Journal,

I have decided I don't need anything. I'm a humble person. For years, I have had the same beautiful quote as a reminder on my desk: "Work Hard, stay humble, and be kind always." I love it. 100% of the profits from this book will be donated to help people and the planet. Split between i=Change, I always wanted to make an impact for all their incredible charities. Ecologi, I didn't get a chance to partner with them to help with all the fantastic climate projects. Now added to my list is a charity very close to my heart, PETA for the animals. Lastly, a charity dealing with domestic and sexual violence, sadly, 1 in 3 women and about 1 in 6 men will experience some form of sexual violence in their lifetime; these are horrific statistics and need to change. I cry with gratitude when I write this entry. This is my biggest passion: to help and make a difference in the world.

Love, Michelle Ashton

Saturday, 9th September 2023

Dear Journal,

I woke up this morning not knowing what to believe anymore. I got home late from the Elvis musical. Oh, 11.15, it was late. I can't keep my eyes open much past 10.30 these days. I pick up my phone and see a group text between myself, my brother, and a phone number that is not in my contacts. I know whose number it is, as it was New Year's Eve, and we discussed the group heading for a late lunch at the restaurant where Adonis was working. It's been on my phone this whole time, and I didn't see it until now. I think is this a sign of Divine timing? Do I reach out with a message? Ok here goes

Hi,

It's been a very long time. Sorry it's late, I just got home from Elvis with my Girlfriend Salma & I realise I am never going to run into you & just be able to say hi.

I really do hope you're doing well?

This Spiritual journey has uncovered some terrifying things for me. I'm totally fine or I will be.

I have changed my phone number so you now have it, if you ever want to say hi. please this is not to be given to absolutely anybody, I'm dead serious. I have warned my brother, he, Salma & my reiki girl are the only ones that have it, none of my other old friends so please keep it to yourself & if you ever want to say hi, you have my number.

Michelle

He asked if it was Michelle, his first wife. I had to stop myself from saying, no, not your first wife; it's your last. We exchanged some words back and forth; it's the only contact I've had with him in months. It feels nice. He makes me feel so calm; he always has.

He told me he had bought a new business, and I was really proud of him. He is such a determined man; it's only been seven months. Everything is nice except for one comment about being so busy working and wanting to be a rich forker. This upsets me; Noah is still operating in the 3D ego-driven world. I am different; money doesn't impress me in the slightest, but kindness does. That's why it's number one on my ideal partner qualities list. All I want to do in this world is help. Don't get me wrong, having a little money to treat yourself occasionally is nice, but that's about it; what else do we really need? I wish everyone could learn from my mistakes. I've been impressed by money before, and look where that got me; money is not what it's about; love is.

Love for ourselves and others; money can't buy love. Maybe Katy from the Quora forum was right, as much as I don't want to acknowledge it. Perhaps this whole journey has just been about Spiritual growth. I so wanted 3D Noah to be his perfect 5D Adonis. I love operating from my 5D; your higher self knows what's best for you. I wish I had known this years ago; I would have saved myself from so much pain and heartache. I speak from experience when I tell you it is worth every tear. I wouldn't go back for any amount of money or fame. I am forever grateful that I have experienced this journey; even though it has been so dark at times, I can finally see the light ahead, and it's so bright.

On another note, every day after I journal, I put the USB inside my safe to guard my mission, and I think how proud I am that that's the only thing in my safe these days!

Love, Michelle Ashton

Sunday, 10th September 2023

Dear Journal,

Today, I went for a massage. The lovely masseuse never asks why my inner thighs are so sore, which is really appreciated. I'm nowhere near ready to talk about it; only my closest and the police know of Horror Night. Afterwards, I sat on a bench outside in the sun, eating my veggie noodles. I saw a pregnant woman. I smile; it feels nice. I can't imagine any time in the near future being able to do that to a man. No way, I don't even want to look them in the eye. After I thought about how much I wanted to be a mum, the pregnant woman seemed so happy. I cried and had to return and sit in the car. It was much easier to process when I thought it was God's will. To think Horror Night was probably the main contributor is too much. I have so much love to give; I always thought what a great mum I would have been; how do I ever reconcile this loss? I can rebuild my life, but that can never be changed or forgotten. I am so upset; everything is overwhelming.

Any small amount of stress feels like it will send me over the edge. I don't want to turn into an angry person. It's tough at the moment. I feel like a zombie most of the time. To try to forget, I went home to lie down and close my eyes for a minute when I got a vision of 3 penises, all sitting in a row. I am made to put my mouth around one and then move on to the next; then I heard the third person say, "Come over here; I need my cock sucked." When will this end? The thoughts and visions are terrifying.

Michelle Ashton

Monday, 11th September 2023

Dear Journal,

It's finally here, the day I get to have my internal ultrasound and X-ray on my shoulder. I'm so happy to start working out some of the issues, but I'm seriously about to pee myself. Then I think that is the least of your worries.

After my appointment, I was eating my veggie bowl when I was guided to see if anyone had published their diary. I googled, and the book "The Diary of Anne Frank" came up. I didn't know of her, but I got chills, especially when I read about her first kiss. I asked the Angels for a sign way back, and was guided to the song One Kiss. Is that who I was in a previous life? I didn't know why I needed to write and document everything; I just did it. I have a knowing it's true. I am honoured to be the one who gets to live out her deepest wishes to become the woman she was meant to become, grow into herself, become a journalist or writer, and write something great.

As I googled for more information, I screamed and cried with joy. Oh my gosh!!!!!!!!!!! I can't stop crying; it's true. I am so honoured and grateful. She chose me; I am her, Annelies Marie Frank. Just as her final entry in The Diary of Anne Frank, our last words are, "As I've told you many times, I'm split in two."

My deepest love and gratitude, Michelle Ashton

www.ingramcontent.com/pod-product-compliance
Lightning Source LLC
Chambersburg PA
CBHW010611100526
44585CB00037B/2491